Competition's New Clothes

Lévêque recounts twenty revealing tales of real-life rivalry between firms across diverse industries, including wine, skiing, opera, video games and cruise liners. These entertaining and insightful narratives are informed by recent advances in economics, factoring in the many forces driving competition, including globalization and innovation. Divided into four sections, the book covers competition and the market; competition and differentiation; competition through innovation; and competition and redistribution. Read together, these stories also serve as building blocks to address the issue of whether competition between firms has entered a new era of increased intensity. This book will appeal anyone, from company executives to consumers, who are interested in the economics of contemporary industry and want to incorporate a grasp of competition into their everyday decision-making. This book can also be used as a supplementary text in courses in microeconomics, business economics and industrial organization.

FRANÇOIS LÉVÊQUE is Professor of Economics at Mines ParisTech, PSL University. He is also a part-time Professor at the Robert Schuman Centre for Advanced Studies, European University Institute, Florence. He founded Microeconomics, a Paris-based economics consultancy, which has recently joined Deloitte.

T0349300

Competition's New Clothes

20 Short Cases on Rivalry Between Firms

FRANÇOIS LÉVÊQUE
Mines ParisTech

CAMBRIDGE
UNIVERSITY PRESS

CAMBRIDGE
UNIVERSITY PRESS

University Printing House, Cambridge CB2 8BS, United Kingdom

One Liberty Plaza, 20th Floor, New York, NY 10006, USA

477 Williamstown Road, Port Melbourne, VIC 3207, Australia

314–321, 3rd Floor, Plot 3, Splendor Forum, Jasola District Centre, New Delhi – 110025, India

79 Anson Road, #06-04/06, Singapore 079906

Cambridge University Press is part of the University of Cambridge.

It furthers the University's mission by disseminating knowledge in the pursuit of education, learning, and research at the highest international levels of excellence.

www.cambridge.org
Information on this title: www.cambridge.org/9781108473590
DOI: 10.1017/9781108562546

© François Lévêque 2019

First published 2019

Printed in the United Kingdom by TJ International Ltd. Padstow Cornwall

A catalogue record for this publication is available from the British Library.

Library of Congress Cataloging-in-Publication Data
Names: Leveque, Francois, author.
Title: Competition's new clothes : 20 short cases on rivalry between firms / Francois Leveque.
Description: New York : Cambridge University Press, 2019.
Identifiers: LCCN 2018036624| ISBN 9781108473590 (hardback) | ISBN 9781108461917 (paperback)
Subjects: LCSH: Organizational behavior. | Competition. | BISAC: BUSINESS & ECONOMICS / Organizational Behavior.
Classification: LCC HD58.7 .L476 2019 | DDC 338.6/048–dc23
LC record available at https://lccn.loc.gov/2018036624

ISBN 978-1-108-47359-0 Hardback
ISBN 978-1-108-46191-7 Paperback

To Didier Pourquery, the editor of my chronicles at The Conversation France, and to Harry Forster, my French-to-English translator.

Contents

Introduction

Competition is extending its reach, growing stronger everywhere. The evidence is there for all to see. Supermarket shelves sag under the weight of goods from all over the world. Neighbourhood stores must compete with online vendors who deliver to our doorstep. The choice of television channels and video content is growing apace. Even electricity and gas monopolies are a distant memory.

But is it really that simple? Giant companies have conquered the planet in leaps and bounds, and now seem unassailable. Big names such as Amazon and Google, of course, but Lego too, in the toy market, or indeed Ikea for home decoration. There are many more, though perhaps as yet little known. Who has ever heard of China Marine International Containers, the world's biggest manufacturer of steel shipping containers? Or Amer Sports, a Finnish concern that leads the market for skis and tennis rackets?

So is competition intensifying or slackening? Is it different in today's global, technology-driven economy than in the past? Hard to say really, so let's look a little closer.

On the one hand, the boundaries of markets are being extended, thanks to the falling costs of transport and communications, which de facto increases the number of competitors serving the same customers. So competition should be greater. On the other hand, markets are shrinking due to growing differentiation of goods and services. Take the example of wine! French wine-growers are now in competition with their counterparts in

Australia and Chile, no longer just with producers in Spain and Italy. Yet, if we set aside the cheapest tipples, wines are far from being interchangeable. The increase in the number of features – be they based on geographic origin, blends of different grape varieties, brands and even terroir – has created myriad micro-markets. Segmented and fragmented in this way, demand faces higher prices. So does competition now work in the same way over markets, which though geographically larger have actually shrunk in marketing terms?

Of course innovation is advancing at a faster pace, disturbing established firms. New entrants have sprung up without warning and are drawing custom away. With its leading position under threat 'old' business has no option but to drop its prices, or follow suit and engage in a headlong race it is far from sure of winning. Yet the economies of scale which characterize research and development, the exclusive rights afforded by intellectual property and the network effects, which attract consumers to one or just a few winners, are all barriers to competition.

Let's examine this contradiction in greater detail, drawing on the example of razors. For many years we watched a battle between two global giants, launching salvoes of multiple-blade cartridges, glide bars and pivoting heads, supported by adverts featuring masculine stars. Then, inspired by Amazon's delivery model and the Netflix subscription scheme, a California-based entrepreneur started offering consumers once-a-month home delivery of basic cartridges at an attractive price. He soon gained millions of subscribers in the USA, ridding them of the tedious and expensive task of stocking up with blades. Now, four years after its launch, the startup has become part of another giant, the Anglo-Dutch firm Unilever.

So the question of novelty and competitive vigour in our modern world certainly demands closer investigation, which is the purpose of this book.

To do so we must observe competition from all angles, sort through various models, follow a pattern, choose the right fabric and, of course, stitch it all together with great care. We must strip competition of its many disguises, the various garbs that hamper our understanding. Only then will we be able to see that it is indeed wearing new clothes, though very much as before.

The Choice of Fabric

There is no better way of understanding competition than by telling stories about it. It is a lively subject and as consumers, employees, managers or entrepreneurs we all have slightly different angles on it. It impinges on us through changes of price and product range, jobs lost here or created there, more or less laborious wage negotiations, shifts in strategy or business model, or indeed the pitfalls and opportunities facing startups.

It is an extremely diverse field. Yet all too often we are presented with some sketchy tale of two companies locked in relentless rivalry: Apple versus Samsung, Boeing and Airbus, General Electric and Siemens, Sotheby's and Christie's. Competition is depicted as a battle between warring giants. When one wins the other loses. This suggests that competition is a zero-sum game, contributing nothing, neither to the protagonists nor, more broadly, to society as a whole. Worse still, as it often gets a bad press, only sordid accounts of industrial break-ins and hold-ups are cited as examples, so competition emerges as an intrinsically negative process.

To fully account for the diverse and subtle ways in which competition acts, I have chosen less exaggerated, more varied examples. They concern a large number of business sectors, industries and markets. They range from the most conventional – shipping and coach transport, consumer goods (such as breakfast cereals and colas) – to the most surprising, notably casino gambling, cruise ships and gyms. But, because they are the best testimony to current trends in competition, I analyse some well-worn topics too, in particular Uber in the field of urban transport and Apple smartphones.

A Four-Part Pattern

The first part in the pattern aims to bring together competition and the market, showing how these two notions are closely connected. Competition operates inside a given geographical area, which may be limited to a city neighbourhood or reach all over the world. So it does not work in the same way between casinos in a specific city as between producers of liquefied-natural gas which ship their product in special ocean-going tankers.

The second part, devoted to competition and differentiation, explains how companies compete by offering differentiated products. This trend has become so widespread that, apart from a few goods such as bananas or salt, it is difficult to find just a single specimen on supermarket shelves. Just think of chocolate or alcoholic beverages. They all differ by at least one feature, such as brand, packaging, origin or ingredients. We live in a massively differentiated world, which makes a huge difference to competition.

The next part, on competition and innovation, takes us into a new world, dominated by smartphones and Internet platforms. Competition has moved away from the solid ground of ordinary rivalry and onto the turbulent, uncertain terrain of uberization, disruptive innovation or indeed creative destruction – with no shortage of terms to describe such processes. The pace of innovation has increased stupendously since the early 1980s and its visible effects on competition are impressive.

The fourth and last part looks at competition and equality. It shows that competition does not have a neutral effect on fairness. Witness the distributive effects of auctioning football broadcasting rights for the benefit of soccer stars, or fixed book prices which penalize the readers of bestsellers. Competition even effects the way profits are shared out between firms, distribution of wealth between consumers and business, and the fate of various categories of consumer. Competition is generally beneficial to society as a whole, but does of course make winners and losers.

Models of Competition

There are many models, for the economic theory of competition does not only concern itself with the number of rival producers. Were that the case the list of such models would be limited to two or maybe three specimens.

The first is fragmented competition, also qualified as perfect, the paragon of market efficiency. It brings into play a host of buyers and sellers trading a strictly identical product, with no power to influence price or the strategy of other parties. At the opposite end of the spectrum the pure monopoly, taking advantage of its position as the market's sole supplier, dictates its (obviously high) price to consumers. This very simplistic dichotomy could be supplemented by the oligopoly, a sort of intermediate case involving a small number of companies. They act on the market price, much as in a monopoly, but are subject to greater constraints, due to the interplay of their respective strategies.

No doubt you are already familiar with this brief list of competition models, but it is very restrictive, reflecting the outlook of nineteenth-century economists. Since then it has grown much longer, so it is high time you came to grips with the advances in the economic theory of competition.

The Fake Clothes of Competition

Let's start by setting aside two misconceptions which plague debate on competition.

The first mistake is to see competition as a universal phenomenon that irrigates every aspect of society, from conjugal competition to rivalry between political parties and leaders, through religious strife. From this point of view there would be no distinction between competition in business, natural selection and sporting contest.

Yet economic competition is a far cry from natural selection, which leads to the strongest eliminating the weakest. Neo-Darwinian biological competition is blind, pitting populations against one another. Moreover, acquired characteristics are not passed on. Competition in industry is also based on chance, if only because it is often underpinned by scientific and technological discoveries. However, unlike plants and most animals, companies made up of men and women carry out deliberate, intentional actions. Competition in this field generally confronts individual firms, not groups of firms, and knowledge and experience are passed on.

Nor is industrial competition comparable to the sporting arena. The latter is a zero-sum game, one player winning, the other losing, with nothing to share between them. The number of players is fixed: two for chess, two teams of 11 players in football, for example. On the other hand, business players are constantly entering and leaving markets, the total number varying because one does not necessarily make up for the other, and companies merge and split up all the time too. Nor are the rules set in stone. Unlike chess-players, rival companies invent new pieces and moves; contrary to football players they choose their playing field and are free to choose means other than just their feet to move the ball.

The second pitfall relates to ideological pre-conceptions and moral judgements. Much as the market, to which it is often likened, competition may give rise to heated debate, degenerating into sweeping statements, the protagonists fighting like cat and dog. Some argue that competition should be encouraged, others that it should be restricted; it is beneficial according to its advocates, devastating in the eyes of its critics. Competition between companies is either demonized or incensed. Depending on one's standpoint, everyone can find economic ideas to fit the bill, some advocating public intervention, others market forces, the State or the 'invisible hand'.

Economists are partly to blame for this stand-off, having long given priority to an exclusively normative approach to competition, using abstract models of general equilibrium and central planning. But in so doing they overlooked the need to study the effects of competition and to understand it as the outcome of market economies. It is the latter, rather more down-to-earth approach that we shall take in this book. We will not be looking at competition from a normative point of view, but that will not stop us outlining elements of economic theory – far from it!

Stripping Away the Trappings of Perfect Competition

The normative approach to the economics of competition has left us with various terms, notably 'perfect competition' and its 'imperfect' opposite, both of which are confusing for non-specialists. It is essential to understand that in practice perfect competition is imperfect and that the equilibrium of perfect competition assumes that there is no competition! Let's start by clarifying these paradoxes.

The first one was pointed out by two leading twentieth-century economists.

Edward Chamberlin asserted that perfect competition diverged from the ideal of perfection, for, were it to exist, it would make us live in a uniform world. Perfect competition is the contrary of variety. We would only be able to buy one type of car, one smartphone, one holiday in the sun.

Joseph Schumpeter maintained that perfect competition would produce a far from ideal world, with neither innovation nor economic progress: no new products the better to satisfy the needs of humankind, no new organization models, no new technology to boost productivity. In short, a stagnant economy quite unlike the perpetual hurricane of creative destruction he saw as the driving force of capitalism.

These two economists also showed that, paradoxically, perfect competition implies the absence of rivalry. In a world of this sort companies and their management would not fight to gain the upper hand, whether this was a matter of developing customer loyalty, raising funds or developing more efficient technology. There would be no sense of emulation. Firms and business leaders would simply adjust their purchases and output to suit market prices, over which they had no control, no more than over demand, through advertising, or production technology, through research and development.

The second paradox of competition without contention is that there are actually two conceptions of competition, which is why it can be both perfect and imperfect at the same time. In fact they are not the same thing! On the one hand competition is seen as an apparently tranquil state of equilibrium in which well-informed economic agents treat prices as parameters. On the other hand it is seen as 'rivalrous behaviour with respect to prices and other variables in a world characterized by flux, uncertainty and disequilibrium'.[1] In one case a situation of stasis, in the other a dynamic process.

It is unfortunate that the two conceptions of competition should be based on a single word, but above all that the term 'imperfect competition' is still in use. Perfect competition is a concept, and as such it is important. But that does not mean its opposite is also a concept. It contributes nothing to our understanding. Economists use this catch-all expression for convenience's sake, to cover all forms of competition in which price is not equal to marginal cost. But this takes many forms and other models can be used to describe their characteristics. Moreover there are differing degrees of competitive imperfection, diverging more or less from a state of equilibrium for a variety of reasons such as asymmetric information between buyers and sellers, or barriers to market entry. The term suggests that competition, if not perfect, should be attacked in all its forms, yet this only holds true for those who wish to live in a motionless, uniform world.

To grasp the novelty and vigour of contemporary competition we must look carefully at its many costumes and how they are cut. All the more so because, though it may change its clothes, they conceal neither its bulk nor its figure. On the contrary a good choice of dress, well cut, shows it off to advantage. All the more so given that such apparel, matching or not, dazzling and colourful, is always better than believing, even for an instant, the competition is wearing clothes so perfect that they are invisible.

Remember the story by Hans Christian Andersen, which you may have read as a child. 'Many years ago, there was an Emperor, who was so excessively fond of new clothes, that he spent all his money in dress. He did not trouble himself in the least about his soldiers; nor did he care to go either to the theatre or the chase, except for the opportunities they afforded him for displaying his new clothes. He had a different suit for each hour of the day.'[2] One day two rogues claimed that they knew how to make clothes with the wonderful property of remaining invisible to everyone who was unfit for the office they held, or who was extraordinarily simple in character. Everyone, including the Emperor, was afraid of being caught out. So they praised the perfect garment till at last a boy shouted out: 'But the Emperor has nothing at all on!'

Notes

1. Vickers, J. (1995), 'Concepts of Competition', *Oxford Economic Papers*, 47(1): 1–23.
2. Project Gutenberg's *Andersen's Fairy Tales*, by Hans Christian Andersen.

PART I

Competition and Market

The merging of the concepts of competition and market was unfortunate, for each deserved a full and separate treatment.
George Stigler, Perfect competition, historically contemplated,
Journal of Political Economy, 1957

Competition is closely connected to a market, in other words to a territory and a product (or service). Competition operates over a given geographic area, which may be as small as a neighbourhood in a big city or encompass the whole world. It works for a specific material good or service sought by corporate customers or final consumers. It makes sense that a ski manufacturer is not competing with a casino operator. Nor for that matter are London cab drivers up against their Parisian counterparts. Moreover, in a given market, competition depends on the number of players with a stake in it. It also makes sense that competition is not as intense when only a few companies are serving a market, rather than a large number. There is less competition in the natural gas market, dominated by just a few firms, than between the dozens of Chinese companies manufacturing freight containers in the 1980s. So as you explore this part, you will learn to distinguish between the market's clothes and those of the competition.

ONE

Three Ski Lessons for Budding Economists

Winter sports may teach us a great deal about the economics of competition. We just need to look at the end of the local monopolies once enjoyed by ski schools, the monopoly power still enjoyed by the suppliers of boots, bindings and boards, and ski lift operators struggling to survive despite the lack of snow. If you reach the end of this series of lessons without taking a tumble, you should qualify for your first star in economics!

Lesson 1. There Are Good and Bad Monopolies

In resorts along the west coast of the United States there is only one ski school offering its services, whether they are large like Vail or more modest in size like Beaver Creek. It enjoys a local monopoly over ski and snowboard lessons. This is surprising in a country that invented anti-trust law! In contrast, in most Italian ski resorts you can choose between several schools, some specializing in a particular approach to tuition, others in a particular discipline, or indeed catering for a certain type of skier. In France, the market is open too, though at first sight it may seem dominated by École de Ski Français (ESF), with its red-suited instructors.

The situation in the USA is an economic anomaly: teaching glide sports is not a natural monopoly. This demands some explanation. It is quite usual for a resort only to have one lift operator,

STVI in Val d'Isère, for instance, because one firm, capturing all of the demand, can offer a service at a lower cost than several firms, among other things due to economies of scale. This property, which economists refer to as the subadditivity of costs, is characteristic of network industries. It would be costly to duplicate Britain's high-voltage power lines or the Channel Tunnel. This natural monopoly is virtuous. All the more so in the case of ski lifts given the pressure on the price of lift passes. The local council or resort developer will be wary, because if lift-pass prices are too high, they will make the resort less attractive, jeopardizing revenue. The lift company must also make allowance for rival services in neighbouring or comparable resorts.

On the other hand there is nothing natural about a monopoly over ski lessons. Even if a ski school enrolled all the potential customers in a resort it wouldn't be able to bring the unit cost of a lesson down any lower than it would be with several ski schools. With only minor fixed costs – reception, nursery-slope equipment and such – economies of scale soon reach their limits. In fact a monopoly of this sort has all sorts of drawbacks. The price of lessons will be higher: adding higher margins, known as monopoly rent, to already higher costs, because, lacking the stimulus of competition, there is no incentive for the monopoly to trim its prices. The quality and range of lessons will suffer too, for the same reason. Glide sports enthusiasts in the USA complain of just these shortcomings. It also explains why there are increasing numbers of freelance instructors in resorts in the Rocky Mountains and why local schools harass them.

Some time ago alternative ski schools such as Evolution 2 or École de Ski Internationale opened in French resorts. This broadened the range of lessons on offer and prompted ESF to pay more attention to customer satisfaction and improve the quality of its own services.

Lesson 2.   Two Monopolies Are Worse than One

Just imagine there is only one manufacturer of bindings in the world and only one ski manufacturer. That would leave consumers facing two monopolies, it being of no use to have skis without bindings, or vice versa. A situation with two consecutive monopolies gave rise to an economic model that is now quite old, but still just as surprising. It dates from 1838 and was posited and demonstrated by Antoine-Augustin Cournot, a French mathematician, economist and thinker. His model predicts that if the two monopolies merge, the overall profit will be greater, but the price of the good will fall, rather than rising. So shareholders and consumers would gain from the operation. The outcome of a merger of our two hypothetical manufacturers would be a retail price for skis lower than the aggregate price of the skis and bindings in the days when they were set separately by the two companies. This counter-intuitive result is easier to understand if you bear in mind that the two monopolies each take a monopoly margin, whereas once they merge only one monopoly margin is left. The merger puts an end to double mark-up.

But what is this model doing here, you may ask. Surely there are plenty of ski manufacturers. True enough, but there aren't that many and above all they sell differentiated products, which gives them monopoly power over their particular market segment. This is admittedly not as great as in a pure monopoly, but sufficient for the Cournot model to hold true.

The top two ski manufacturers, Amer Sports and Jarden, share about half the market, though you probably aren't familiar with their names. They are large, diversified corporations which own many brands (Salomon, Atomic, Dynamic and Arc'Teryx in the first case; K2, Völkl, Marker and Dalbello in the second). They are followed by firms that specialize in mountain sports gear but also own several brands: Rossignol, which controls Dynastar, Lange, Kerma and Look; Tecnica, which controls Nordica, Blizzard and Moon Boot.

There is obviously more to differentiating skis than just the brand name. France's Vieux Campeur sports retailer features 100 different models in its catalogue, and that's just in the downhill ski section. Two economists who have studied the diversity of these products, identified more than 500 models on offer in the European market.[1] They differ in many ways: technical characteristics (material, weight, carving radius, and such); use (giant slalom, downhill, off-piste, etc.); type of skier (beginner, expert, competition); and appearance (colour and design, among others). The price range is just as large. Such differentiation enables manufacturers to avoid head-on competition, giving each one some monopoly, or market, power, each model being to some extent unique.

The ski manufacturing industry has undergone a series of mergers and acquisitions by diversification. Some firms wanted to achieve growth by taking over another firm's business: ski manufacturers bought out binding manufacturers (Rossignol acquired Look in 1994) or boot manufacturers (Rossignol acquired Lange in 1989); conversely boot manufacturers bought the makers of skis (Tecnica acquired Nordica in 2003, then Blizzard in 2006); binding manufacturers joined forces with their counterparts in skis (Head and Tyrolia in 1985); and ski manufacturers even took control of pole makers (Dynastar bought Kerma in 1987). All these operations spared the consumer a succession of mark-ups. Nowadays most firms producing winter sports gear offer skis, bindings and boots, which suits consumers better. (They have also diversified into many other goods, such as skiwear, tennis rackets and football boots, but the purpose of this sort of integration is not to end double mark-up, because purchases of these goods by consumers are not necessarily linked.)

Lesson 3. Entry, Exit and Trickery

To understand competition the budding economist may be tempted to focus on competition in more familiar fields such as biology or sport. But with a better grasp of the basics they will see that it takes a different form in economics. That being as it may, such parallels may prove instructive at this stage.

Much as with the evolution of a species, we see companies entering and exiting the market. They may be studied using survival models, statistical instruments that identify and measure the factors determining the failure of a business. They reveal several trends. For example, the likelihood that a company will survive increases with its age, but decreases as an industry ages. The former result suggests that the first market entrants are more efficient, which may be explained by learning economies. The older a company, the more it has produced; the more it produces, the better it is at producing; and the better it is at producing, the lower its unit cost. The latter result suggests that the efficiency threshold which a viable venture must attain rises with time, which may be due to technological progress.

Survival analysis has been applied to ski lift operators in Austria.[2] In the past twenty years, almost one in ten have stopped trading, along with the ski area they were serving. Predictably, high-altitude resorts stand a better chance of survival. Other things being equal, the likelihood of failure is six times lower above 1,700 metres. The absence of a nearby resort, which would cause local competition attracting skiers, also impacts favourably on the likelihood of survival. Less predictably, the econometric model shows that the ski areas standing a better chance of survival were among the first to install snow cannons. However this finding agrees with the theory that innovative firms have a higher chance of survival. In passing, we should point out that fitting artificial snow equipment is not a catch-all solution for resorts to adapt to the effects of climate change, particularly small ones located at low altitudes. A recent survey of resorts in the French Alps estimates that almost a third of the surface area of ski slopes is equipped with snow cannons and this figure doesn't vary much between different types of resort.[3] On the other hand, projects to extend artificial snow cover by 2020 are restricted to large, high-altitude locations, the aim being to achieve 50% coverage. Artificial snow requires substantial investment, is expensive to produce and only achieves the desired result at low temperatures.

Drawing a parallel between industrial and sporting competition highlights common ground: in either case it is a matter of winning by merit, not cheating. Athletes must go by the rule book and not resort to doping; companies must obey the law, in particular upholding consumer rights and competition law. The latter does not prohibit dominant and monopoly positions as such, only abusive action to achieve or maintain such advantage. Which is just as well for the economy, for obtaining or maintaining market power is the prime incentive for firms to cut costs and improve the quality of their products. But just as for athletes they must prevail on merit and not resort to abusive practices that eliminate competitors or deceive consumers. For instance, in the USA, the Federal Trade Commission's Bureau of Competition ruled against Marker Völkl and Tecnica.[4] The two competitors had agreed not to solicit, call or recruit professional skiers who had already signed an endorsement agreement with the other party, in other words, a non-compete agreement that increased their chances of retaining star skiers without their cost increasing.

Misleading advertising on product quality with the intent to fool consumers is also subject to prosecution. One amusing example concerns exaggerated reports of snow falls in ski resorts. Over several years, two US researchers compared snow falls as reported by the national weather service and self-reported by resorts, via their websites.[5] They found that the resorts announced more days with falls of over 20 centimetres of snow than the government service, and fewer days with no snow at all. The depth of snow claimed by the resorts was 15% greater than recordings by the public service. As these results could have been due to a difference between local observation points for the two sources of information, the authors checked for any variation depending on the day of the week. The divergence between reported and self-reported snow falls increased on Saturdays and Sundays. According to the resorts' websites it snowed more at weekends than on other days of the week. This meteorological oddity is not surprising in economic terms, there being a greater incentive for resorts to embellish reality at weekends in order to attract skiers for the two-day break; visitors staying for a whole week buy their pass when they arrive. Furthermore, weekend divergences were greater at resorts with another resort less than 80 kilometres away. This sort of practice is obviously not consistent with efforts to attract skiers on merit alone!

Congratulations! You've reached the end of this series of lessons for beginners. If you read it all in one go, you deserve your first star for economics.

Notes

1. Corrocher, N. and Guerzoni, M. (2009), 'Product variety and price strategy in the skimanufacturing industry', *Journal of Evolutionary Economics*, 19: 471–486.
2. Falk, M. (2013), 'A survival analysis of ski lift companies', *Tourism Management*, 36: 377–390.
3. François, H., George-Marcelpoil, E., Morin, S. and Spandre, P. (2015), 'Dynamique de la neige de culture dans les Alpes Françaises', *Journal of Alpine Research*, 103: 1–19.
4. 'Two companies are barred from non-compete agreements', Federal Trade Commission press release, 9 May 2014.
5. Zinman, J. and Zitzewitz, E. (2016), 'Wintertime for deceptive advertising?', *Applied Economics*, 8: 177–192.

TWO

Containers Conquering the World

Freight containers have changed the face of the world. By cutting the cost of goods transport this key twentieth-century innovation has made the planet a smaller place and extended the global economy.[1] Yet they are very simple objects: a corrugated-steel box, 20 feet long, 8.5 wide and 8 high, fitted with a double door and a plywood floor. Stacked one on top of another on quaysides or cargo ships, they form gigantic, multicoloured walls.

There are currently almost 40 million units. If you want to buy one new, to use it as a garage or as student accommodation at the bottom of the garden, it will cost less than $2,000 at the factory gate. The price is in dollars because, much as a barrel of Brent crude oil, standard containers are bought and sold in American currency. They are a commodity, a basic product with no differentiation, its standard characteristics familiar to buyers and sellers.[2] Economic theory long ago established the properties of competitive commodity markets: a known price that applies to all parties, determined by marginal cost and subject to considerable fluctuation, going up and down like a roller-coaster. Crude oil, natural gas, soy beans, sugar and steel are usually cited as illustrations of these properties.

The Standard Container Is a Commodity

The twenty-foot shipping container is a fine example too. In the 1980s, dozens of firms in China started manufacturing them. With limited needs in the way of technology or skills, low labour costs and a prime location close to a new market – fed by the boom in Chinese exports – these companies prospered. Surfing on rising demand, they initially enjoyed comfortable profit margins. But the picture changed when the market began to slow down in the 1990s. Competition on prices was relentless. The market value of freight containers plummeted, manufacturers with high overheads shut up shop while others, in a bid to survive, desperately cut costs. They resorted to a whole range of measures to improve efficiency: optimizing manufacturing processes; rationalizing procurement; comparing the performance of factories; streamlining the logistics of customer deliveries; gaining access to low-cost capital, and so on. The first decade of the new century witnessed a similar cycle, reaching a low point in 2002 with the price of a container pegged at $1,350, then peaking at $2,350 in 2008, only to plummet again as the financial crisis kicked in. After a brief recovery, the price of shipping containers once more slumped in the early 2010s as Chinese exports and global growth slowed.

Roller-Coaster Price Fluctuations

The economic theory of commodities explains such volatility. The equilibrium price – situated at the point where the supply and demand curves intersect – peaks when customer demand is high and production capacity saturated. Under these conditions the curves rise almost vertically, intersecting high in the sky. With a production plant working flat out, the cost of producing any additional units is prohibitive. After all, what can one do when stocks run out? Restart outdated production lines that are catastrophically inefficient? Or push machinery beyond its limits, with the risk of wrecking it? Such short-term expedients are costly. So when production capacity is saturated, the supply side is almost completely insensitive to price fluctuations.

On the demand side this is almost always the case. A commodity is an essential good for manufacturing other goods and services, so the volume of demand does not vary very much with price. At the other end of the scale, the equilibrium price plunges at times of surplus capacity and flagging demand. The curves intersect way down, in the almost horizontal part of the supply curve, which has become very elastic to price. At such times manufacturers can adjust output depending on its cost compared with a market price which applies to all players. If that price dips below a manufacturer's marginal cost – or, to put it more simply, below their operating cost – they will reduce output, because they are making a loss. On the other hand, if the price is just slightly higher that their marginal cost, they can increase output, because they are making money. They will do this even if their margin is too slight to cover fixed costs or, in simpler terms, pay off the cost of investments.

So much for the formation of short-term prices in commodity markets, short-term in this context referring to the time needed for new capacity to be rolled out or for technological progress.[3] So the means of production and level of technology are fixed, whether we are dealing with the area of land being farmed and its output, or the number of oil wells and extraction processes.

Almost Perfect Competition?

Modelling long-term price dynamics is much trickier. We must juggle with a larger number of parameters, such as macro-economic and geo-political conditions. Furthermore, economic agents are no longer passive; they do not just set their output volume as a function of the market price. They may, for instance, decide to invest in research and development, and build additional capacity. So economic theory seeks to understand successive cycles as prices soar then plummet in an effort to predict the next boom, or bust.

The lower part of the first cycle in China's container market is interesting as a good example of almost perfect competition. The conditions for the model of perfect competition – so often repeated in economics classes, so rarely observed in practice – were more or less fulfilled: a large number of manufacturers and customers, easy entry to and exit from the industry, homogeneous product, freely available information, mobility of production factors.

But the example is no longer valid; almost perfect competition in the container business is ancient history. One firm, China International Marine Containers (CIMC), now dominates the market and the barriers to entry are very high. Half of all containers manufactured worldwide are made in a CIMC plant. In the 1980s, it produced about 10,000 containers a year, much as its competitors. Its largest factory, in Shenzhen, now produces 30 times that amount. However unglamorous containers may seem, CIMC now makes an ideal case study for MBA students wishing to understand how to conquer a commodity market by cost-innovation and international growth. Once it had gained control of its home territory, in particular by buying up the production plant of bankrupt competitors at knock-down prices, CIMC leveraged its lower costs to oust many of its rivals in Japan and South Korea. An additional factor in its favour was that its rivals often belonged to conglomerates: if recurrent estimates of the value of their business portfolio reveal a deficit, or even a meagre profit, on container manufacturing, they will sooner or later cut their losses and axe the business.

The Case of CIMC

CIMC subsequently improved the quality of its product and diversified. Customers can now find more technically sophisticated containers. Some have odd dimensions, like the 53-footer ubiquitous in North America. Others fold to take up less space when empty (as on the journey back to China). Then there are refrigerated containers, for transporting fruit, vegetables or meat, not to mention tank-containers for shipping liquids such as wine or hydrogen peroxide. There are even Aquaviva containers for carrying live lobsters in their natural sea-water environment. CIMC produces trailers for trucks, straddle carriers and cranes for ports, gangways and steps for loading aircraft, among others. The world's second largest container manufacturer, Singamas, lags far behind, reporting sales seven times lower. It holds a 20% market share. And guess what! It's another Chinese firm. But unlike its rival, Singamas has scarcely ventured beyond the freight-container market.

One Player Accounting for Half of Global Output

As far as I know, no economists have analysed the formation of current short-term prices in the shipping-container market. But there seems good reason to suppose that, with a firm grip on half of global output, CIMC can now influence prices. The Chinese firm can prevent market cycles dipping too deep and keeping prices sufficiently high not only to cover its short-term marginal costs but also to show a decent return on investment. It can adjust capacity quickly, because the production cycle for containers is a great deal shorter than in the past. It holds a position similar to the one that Aramco, Saudi Arabia's state oil monopoly, would enjoy if it owned all the capacity in the Arabian Gulf. It is less certain that CIMC can abuse its position to push prices further up when they peak in response to strong demand. Indeed, its main shareholder, China Cosco Shipping, is one of the world's leading container shipping companies.

Other shipping companies have interests in container manufac-turing. Buyers would obviously rather price volatility remains within reasonable limits. So the fluctuations in the price of twenty-foot containers are likely to flatten out to some extent. Prices will probably come into line with costs, in other words all overheads and return on investment. But they will fluctuate even so, if only to keep pace with the price of steel, the main item of expenditure when manufacturing a freight container, steel being a commodity too and subject to price volatility.

Incidentally, when Franco-Chinese artist Huang Yongping did a show at the Grand Palais, Paris, in 2016, he built an aluminium serpent over 200 metres long undulating over stacks of shipping containers looking very much like a roller-coaster!

Notes

1. Levinson, M. (2006), *The Box: How the Shipping Container Made the World Smaller and the World Economy Bigger*, Princeton, NJ: Princeton University Press.
2. Giraud, P.-N. and Ollivier, T. (2015), *L'Économie des Matières Premières*, Paris: Éditions La Découverte.
3. Giraud and Ollivier, *L'Économie des Matières Premières*, ibid.

THREE

Casinos and One-Armed Bandits

Slot machines, much as lotteries, are games of pure chance. But that doesn't stop punters, who believe in luck and illusory forms of causality. They think, for example, they're more likely to win on their birthday and can make up their losses by playing for a longer time. Nor does it stop economists from taking an interest in casinos, just like any other industry.

What Price Gaming?

In the old days when you pulled the single lever on a slot machine, you would hear coins cascading down. Now you just press a button and payment is made electronically, but if you play a very large number of times the machine will still rob you, just as before. So if you only gamble to make money, it's better to avoid slot machines, and if you go to Las Vegas for fun, don't go straight for the one-armed bandits at the airport. The price of gambling there is higher than in town. Price, what price, I hear you say. It isn't displayed anywhere, unlike the goods on sale in the duty-free stores and eateries in the terminals. Moreover, unlike other pastimes such as seeing a movie, it's not an easy idea to grasp. Is it the amount spent per hour working the slots? The average value of bets placed in each game? Remarkably enough, the price here is not actually expressed as money but as a percentage. Specialists in the economics of gambling obtain an approximate price from the proportion of wagers paid back to gamblers in wins. The 'return to player' is around 85% at McCarran compared to about 90% in casinos in the city. In other words you lose about 15 cents to the dollar playing at the airport, compared to about 10 cents in Las Vegas. So the price of gambling on slot machines is defined as the percentage of the money wagered which the owner of the machine keeps: 15% at the airport, in the present instance, or 10% in the city.

Several clues suggest that consumers are sensitive to this price, despite it not being apparent. The pioneer of gambling studies, economist W. R. Eadington, cites this amusing example, which will come as no surprise if you've played roulette on both sides of the Atlantic.[1] In Europe the wheel has 37 pockets and you can bet on 36 numbers, from one to thirty-six. If the ball stops on zero, the bank wins. In the United States, the ball can end up in any one of 38 pockets, there being a double-zero spot, also for the bank. However, as in Europe, if your number comes up you will win 35 times what you wagered. The price of roulette in the USA is therefore 5.2% (or 2/38), as against 2.7% (1/37) in Europe. Given this price, which is almost twice as high, fewer gamblers opt to play roulette in US casinos.

Similarly the price of one-armed bandits is higher in casinos which mainly attract tourists than in the ones with regular, locally based customers. The latter are more price-conscious: gambling more frequently they have a better grasp of price and word-of-mouth works better between them.

Competition and Price

A word of warning, though: the above observation only holds true for an identical competitive situation. Given that casinos with a local customer base tend to be more isolated in their catchment area, whereas casinos targeting visitors are often located close to one another on the same thoroughfare, the higher price charged in the first case may also be due to less intense competition. The effect of competition on price is immediately apparent if one compares lotteries with casinos. Française des Jeux, the successor of the Loterie Nationale, enjoys a monopoly over scratchcards and lottery draws, whereas there are several firms operating casinos, which in some areas are quite close. Witness the French Riviera. In casinos, the return to player is 85% – so the price is 15% – compared with 65%, or a price of 35%, for the national lottery.[2]

Other examples endorse this finding. At the end of the 1990s, the price of gambling at Las Vegas, where there were nearly 100 casinos, was 5.1%. At Atlantic City, New Jersey, with only about a dozen venues, it was half as much again.[3] In Iowa and states bordering on it, the fivefold rise in the number of casinos in the 1990s brought the price down from 10% to 6%.[4]

Of course competition between casinos also hinges on many other factors: the range of games on offer, particularly table games – roulette, baccarat, poker and such – even if casinos earn most of their revenue from slot machines; the décor and interior design, as we might surmise from the title of a book by a specialist consultant, *Designing Casinos to Dominate the Competition*[5]; or the catering and hotel services on hand, among others. None of this will come as a surprise if you gamble and have already been to Las Vegas. Indeed one is tempted to say that competition focuses mainly on factors other than price. Consumers are quick to notice them. There is some competition on price but it is necessarily slight.

Territorial Competition

Both of the term's meanings are relevant here: competition between territories to set up casinos; and competition between casinos established on the same territory. The first instance concerns local authorities, which see such businesses as a source of economic growth and even more surely revenue. In the second instance companies compete with one another for the prime location and how best to attract custom to their venue.

Let's look at this two-pronged competition in the light of what has happened in the USA. For a long time gambling was prohibited everywhere, except Nevada. Only bingo was tolerated. It was organized by churches and charities, so its social side justified allowing it. Revenue was used for a good cause and it was an opportunity for otherwise isolated folk to meet. There was a time in California when the legislation was so strict that it was forbidden even to play poker at home on the kitchen table or in the lounge.

That all changed towards the end of the twentieth century and only a small number of states – such as Utah, subject to Mormon influence – now ban gambling. In twenty to thirty years the USA has become a paradise for slot-machine addicts.

The Race to Legalize Gambling

Such developments in the USA have been a boon for econometrists too. The rate at which prohibition has been lifted in the different states has varied, so the country displays a diversity of contexts ideal for econometrics. It shows that competition between states has given rise to a form of cannibalization. With legalization the first casinos were often established close to interstate borders, particularly in corners. It's not because gambling is forbidden in one state that its residents can't enjoy some fun in a neighbouring state where it's allowed. But the loss of fiscal revenue from its residents in state A becomes an incentive for it too to legalize gambling. Three US econometrists showed that it was more likely for a state to legalize gaming on its territory if a neighbouring state had already taken the plunge and, other things being equal, it would do so sooner, compared to the situation without a neighbouring state that had legalized gambling.[6] In short, legalization of gambling has started a race between states and the number of casinos all over the

USA has substantially increased. Initially the outcome of such competition was a positive-sum game, with increased spending on slot machines. In other words, betting in the new casinos of state A exceeded the dip in expenditure in the casinos of state B, which legalized gambling first. The rise in the number of casinos fuelled demand for slot machines. The same applied to fiscal revenue: state A gained some, its neighbour lost some, but the aggregate was positive.

It now seems to have become a zero-sum game. Building new casinos and adding to the number of slot machines no longer increases overall demand. In some areas, competition has even turned into a destructive, negative-sum game. In the Mid-Atlantic region (which includes New Jersey in particular) with Pennsylvania entering the fray, and the subsequent rise in the number of casinos, aggregate revenue for the region as a whole has dropped. One explanation[7] that has been aired is that Pennsylvania punters gamble less close to home than they did when they had to travel 60 or 70 miles before hitting the slots. Under the circumstances, it made sense to play for longer and lay higher bets once they reached their destination!

Cannibalization can jeopardize the lottery too. Econometric analysis has shown that for every additional dollar spent on the slots in Pennsylvania, betting on the lottery falls by between 5 and 15 cents.[8]

Spatial Competition Between Casinos

Keener competition between states is exacerbating spatial competition (see Chapter 10) between casinos, for as their number has increased, the distance between them has shrunk. A larger number of gamblers can thus choose between several venues to work the slots. Research has shown that in the Mid-West spending on these machines for a given venue dropped by about one-third for every ten additional casinos in its area.[9] In Missouri, a 10% increase in competitive intensity, measured according to the number of machines in the vicinity, led to a 5.7% cut in the value of wagers in a specific casino.[10]

So the distance between a specific venue and surrounding casinos impacts on its takings, due to two contrary forces. One, which is intuitive, is linked to the loss of custom as the number of rival casinos rises. The other, perhaps less obvious, is due to a positive aggregate effect: the more casinos there are in the neighbourhood, the more attractive the destination becomes. Just think of Las Vegas, which attracts hordes of visitors from far and wide to have a flutter and lose some money. Moreover, spatial competition does not only operate locally. The rise of Atlantic City exerted downward pressure on demand for gaming at Las Vegas.[11] The boom in the fortunes of Macau, which in just a few years has become a prime international destination, has very probably had a similar impact. If you live in Europe the distance to Macau or Vegas is pretty much the same, and both boast a miniature Venice and a toy Eiffel tower. If you're in any doubt as to which one to choose, you could always toss a coin!

Notes

1. Eadington, W. R. (1999), 'The economics of casino gambling', *The Journal of Economic Perspectives*, 13: 173–192.
2. Rakedjian, E. and Robin, M. (2014), 'Les jeux d'argent en France', *Insee Première*: 1493.
3. Eadington, 'The economics of casino gambling', ibid.
4. Ali, M. and Thalheimer, R. (2003), 'The demand for casino gaming', *Applied Economics*, 35: 907–918.
5. Friedman, B. (2000), *Designing Casinos to Dominate the Competition*, Institute for the Study of Gambling and Commercial Gaming.
6. Condliffe, S. (2012), 'Pennsylvania casinos' cannibalization of regional gambling revenues', *UNLV Gaming Research & Review Journal*: 45–58.
7. Ibid.

8. Economopoulos, A. J. and Stolle, W. (2012), 'Do Pennsylvania casinos cannibalize PA state lottery revenues?', *Business and Economic Faculty Publications*.
9. Ali and Thalheimer, (2003). 'The demand for casino gaming'. *Applied Economics*, 35(8), 907–918.
10. Nesbit, T. M. and Walker, D. M. (2014), 'Casino revenue sensitivity to competing casinos: a spatial analysis of Missouri', *Growth and Change*, 45: 21–40.
11. Shonkwiler, J. (1992), 'A structural time series model of Nevada gross taxable gaming revenues', *The Review of Regional Studies*, 22: 239–249.

FOUR

The Great Game of International Gas

At present, if you live in Europe, the gas burning in your boiler or stove may come from the Urals, but in the near future it might come from the United States. The same applies to electricity: some is generated using Russian gas, but power plants in the European Union may soon be burning American shale gas. Gazprom, the EU's top supplier, is far from happy about this prospect. Nor is the Kremlin, which pulls the strings at the gas conglomerate. Welcome to the great game of global gas!

The World as It Was

For a long time, natural gas was only transported in pipes, a far cry from the huge quantities now shipped in special tankers. Liquid natural gas (LNG) consists mainly of methane, or CH_4, with one carbon atom and four hydrogen atoms, the shortest and lightest hydrocarbon molecule, as you may recall from your chemistry classes. You probably also know that methane can be converted into a liquid, taking up several hundred times less space than it does as a gas. This is obviously more convenient for shipping, even if the tankers resemble giant floating freezers, for LNG must be kept at $-163°C$! Of course on arrival, the same process must be reversed, converting the methane back into a gas that can be transported in the usual way by pipe.

Even longer ago, the gas we consumed was not extracted direct from the subsoil but obtained from coal. The historical primacy of gas manufactured to light towns explains why we now refer to natural gas, whereas we would never think of saying 'natural oil' or 'natural bauxite'.

For many years, there was nothing to compete with natural gas (apart from other energy sources, particularly coal and crude oil). To simplify matters very slightly, a sole national gas company in each European country took care of the entire supply chain, from transport in large and then smaller pipes, through to sales to end users. In some cases, this even included production, as was the case in Holland. In France, however, Elf Aquitaine produced gas at Lacq, south of Bordeaux, and Gaz de France handled everything else. Failing domestic resources, or to supplement them, the national company would purchase gas from one or more supplier(s), also state owned, such as Sonatrach in Algeria or Gazprom.

In the case of a single seller and a single buyer, two monopolies come face to face. For a long time, economists disliked this situation, termed a bilateral monopoly, because it did not lead to market equilibrium. Unlike conditions of perfect competition, a basic monopoly or an oligopoly, in a bilateral monopoly there is nothing obliging either party to set a fixed quantity or price. There are several solutions – indeed an infinite number – the outcome depending on which party is in the strongest position. If the buyer has the most bargaining power, the price will be low. Alternatively, if the seller holds the upper hand, the price will be high.

Bilateral Monopoly

For a long time even the finest economists[1] were stumped by bilateral monopolies and the leading microeconomics textbooks set forth erroneous solutions.[2] In fact an equilibrium quantity can be found for trade between the two parties. To be optimal, this quantity must maximize joint profit, in other words the profit made if the two companies operated as a single entity. On the other hand, there is no equilibrium price for the intermediate good. The price simply reflects the agreement reached by the two parties on how to share the joint profit. It is a sort of transfer price between two separate companies, which negotiate and co-ordinate their business.

What's more, the consumer couldn't care less about the price of the intermediate good. Just imagine, in the world we once knew, the customers of Gaz de France, a monopoly in those days supplied exclusively by its Russian counterpart. All the consumer had to worry about was whether the amount of gas coming across the border, determined by the two parties, was equal or close to the optimum. Since Augustin Cournot (see Chapter 1) economic theory has shown that if two companies maximize their joint profit, then the price of the end product, which the consumer pays, will be the most advantageous one for the latter.

But was that actually the case at the time? Even now, with the benefit of hindsight, it's hard to say because there are few instances of a 'pure' bilateral monopoly and the historical data on quantities and prices are still confidential. For many years, trade between two parties was exclusively governed by long-term contracts to which only they were privy. This was before the start of free gas markets managed by stock markets. For twenty years or more, such contracts set a minimum quantity which the buyer had to take regardless of the circumstances and a price consisting of a constant term and a series of indexation parameters, in particular the exchange rate and the price of crude oil. To keep things simple, under these 'take or pay' contracts, the buyer took charge of the volume risk and the seller took charge of the price risk, by insuring that gas remained competitive with other fuels. Without knowing the terms of such contracts, it is impossible to establish retrospectively whether the price negotiated by the two parties coincided with the theoretical model, nor yet which of them took the lion's share of the joint profit.

Gazprom Versus the EU?

Do you remember the winter of 2008–2009? After an early start, it turned bitterly cold. Temperatures in January were the lowest for twenty years. That was the winter when Russia decided, for reasons both political and financial, to cut off the supply of gas at its border with Ukraine, which was no longer paying its debts. For two weeks at the beginning of the year it stopped all deliveries. Ukraine just happens to be a key location for the transit of Russian gas on its way to the EU. The people of south-eastern Europe suffered a great deal from the stoppage, being almost exclusively dependent on Russian gas for heating and generating electricity. Tens of thousands of people were deprived of energy and left to freeze. This crisis strengthened the EU's determination to take action to diversify its sources of supply for gas and bolster energy-security policy.

Previously it focused mainly on opening its markets to competition and streamlining trade between countries in the economic community. This ambitious undertaking undermined the monopoly position of incumbent national gas suppliers and tightened control over interconnection infrastructure linking member states. Taking a closer look, this entailed a lot of technical measures: vertical separation between the management of pipelines and the gas they carry; regulation of transport networks; launch of gas spot markets. It went hand-in-hand with constant criticism of long-term contracts. Brussels saw their duration as an obstacle to new entrants, dismissed the indexation formula linking them to the price of crude oil as having no economic basis, and condemned them overall as incompatible with EU law in so far as they prevented a buyer in a member state from reselling imported gas to a fellow operator in another member state.

Or the EU Versus Gazprom?

In other words, EU policy on energy security and market liberalization did not – and still does not – suit Gazprom. Lets look at two sources of irritation, in particular.

Just off the coast of Lithuania is a floating regasification terminal to process gas arriving by tanker, particularly from Norway. This investment, assisted by Brussels, has enabled the Baltic state to reduce its physical and economic dependence on Russian gas delivered overland. The facility provides the country with an alternative point of entry for importing gas. Furthermore, even if it is not yet operating at full capacity, it is putting competitive pressure on Gazprom, forcing it to drop its price.

Another source of irritation is the destination clause which prevents reselling to other member states. This clause allows Gazprom to set different prices from one country to the next. This is justified by the need to adapt local conditions regarding the competitive advantage of gas over oil, but in practice it leads to prices which bear no relation to the distance from the Russian border, or in other words the cost of transporting the gas. For example the price of Russian gas in Germany, despite it being closer to the Urals than France, has long been higher than in the latter country. This means that Gazprom can discriminate against consumers depending on their geographical origin. It should be borne in mind that discriminatory strategy always favours a monopoly, because the profits earned with prices that make allowance for varying consumer demands are higher than if customers all pay the same price. However, willingness to pay for gas still depends on many national characteristics such as the price end users pay for oil and the various types of equipment used for central heating and generating electricity. So if the ban on reselling is lifted, geographical discrimination would no longer be possible, meaning a drop in Gazprom's profits.

The most recent episode in the shifting tensions between Gazprom and the European Commission started in April 2015. This time the game featured two big hitters, both with a background in economics. On one side of the table was Margrethe Vestager, the competition commissioner, who purportedly served as inspiration for the Danish TV series Borgen. Opposite her was Alexander Medvedev, deputy-chairman of Gazprom's management committee and former president of the Kontinental Hockey League. A week after launching an attack on Google, Vestager alleged that the Russian conglomerate was abusing its dominant market position in the eastern part of the EU. She asserted that in eight member states Gazprom was obstructing reselling of gas and imposing unfair prices. Since then the two parties have come to terms. The Commission has obtained an end to territorial restrictions, but Gazprom has avoided a fine which could have amounted to several billion euros.

The Great Reconfiguration

This title, borrowed from a book edited by two gas experts, suggests that the European gas game is no longer limited to just the EU and its neighbours – the three gas exporting countries Algeria, Norway and Russia.[3] This claim is based on the fact that LNG is increasingly being shipped by special tankers from terminals in the USA and Australia.

To cut a long story short, gas is temporarily over-abundant, though no one can say how long this situation may last. Growth in demand is lower than forecast. Meanwhile competition from coal, particularly in Asia, and renewables, in Europe, has stiffened. At the same time capacity – for production, liquefaction-regasification and marine transport – has substantially increased.

The tankers sailing from US ports are primarily stocked with shale gas. Originally these ports were geared to unloading, rather than loading gas. The boom in home-grown gas has reversed the flow.

On the coast, massive regasification plants used to turn the hydro-carbon from liquid to gas, so that it could be conveyed inland by pipeline. They have now been rejigged to do the opposite, liquefying shale gas for export. This represents a considerable outlay, but the cost is lower than building liquefaction plants from scratch. In Australia, new production and liquefaction capacity is also coming online. Over the next five years these two countries will account for 90% of growth in LNG exports.

But Where Will All the Ships Go?

Once on board, liquefied gas can go anywhere, bearing in mind that shipping costs do nevertheless increase with distance. So Australian LNG tankers will go to Asia, their traditional market, that continent being closest. On leaving Australian ports, the cost of the gas is already high. Transporting the stuff over long distances would further add to the cost.

US tankers have more leeway. The costs of extracting non-conventional gas in the USA are low; an impressive network of pipelines criss-crosses the whole country; and markets such as Henry Hub, the best known of all, are extremely efficient. Above all, a new business model has been invented for the liquefaction trains. These huge facilities no longer belong to gas producers but to independent companies, which make ends meet by charging their customers a fixed fee. This is a form of rent, being due even if an exporter ultimately decides not to liquefy a single cubic metre of gas. In this way, the plant owner avoids any risk due to the volatility of gas prices and firms using the facility can limit losses if the export market suffers a downturn. The absence of a destination clause is another exceptional feature of this model. Once on board, the owner of the shipment can choose where it will be delivered. To nearby South America, to not-so-distant Europe or even faraway Asia. Deliveries to the latter market are now economically viable and technically feasible for tankers which mostly fill up on the coast of the Gulf of Mexico. Work widening the Panama Canal has recently been completed, avoiding a long and tiresome journey through the Suez Canal or round the Cape of Good Hope.

Up till now, US LNG tankers have above all sailed to South America. The trip to Europe is not much longer but in Brazil or Argentina there is no competition for LNG from gas transported overland by pipeline. It's essential to bear in mind that the cost of liquefaction, marine transport and regasification is twice that of transporting methane overland. So far only two LNG tankers from the USA have delivered a shipment to a European port, and only one has docked in China.

The globalization of gas markets is underway and it doesn't suit Gazprom at all.

Notes

1. Machlup, F. and Taber, M. (1960), 'Bilateral monopoly, successive monopoly, and vertical integration', *Economica*, 27: 101–119.
2. Blair, R. D., Kaseman, D. L. and Romano, R. E. (1999), 'A pedagogical treatment of bilateral monopoly', *Southern Economic Journal*, 55: 831–841.
3. Corbeau, A-S. and Ledesma, D. (eds) (2016), *LNG Markets in Transition: The Great Reconfiguration*, Oxford: Oxford University Press.

FIVE

The Glamorous Shipping Market

What could be less glamorous, more humdrum, than a regular shipping service? Tens of thousands of container ships tirelessly move goods from one port to another across the world. They sail on time and dock at their destination several days or weeks later, steaming gently but steadily at a speed of 15 to 20 knots. Few accidents upset the tranquil existence of these ocean-going giants, though they do occasionally spill their cargo of metal boxes onto a beach somewhere. The economics of container ships, in contrast, is much more agitated. Moreover, it is a source of controversy centring on notions of destructive competition and beneficial cartel, oxymorons that set our theoretical compasses spinning.

Bigger Container Ships

The maritime transport of containers is carried out by companies offering a regular service at set dates along a fixed route. For instance a CMA-CGM vessel will leave Shanghai on 28 September docking in Rotterdam on 25 October. It doesn't matter if the goods you're importing from China aren't ready. One of this company's ships sails every Sunday and vessels operated by other companies leave on other days of the week. Although it is a service and not a product, regular shipping is also a commodity (see Chapter 2). Competition between firms hinges on price and only price, so the pressure on cutting costs is relentless.

To cut the cost per container, shipyards are busy building bigger vessels. Container ships have doubled in size over the past ten years, an increase that far outstrips the growth of any other type of vessel. The largest of all, Maersk's Triple E class, dwarfs even the biggest oil tankers. Four hundred metres long, it can carry up to 18,000 containers, also known as twenty-foot equivalent units (TEUs). Expressed in other terms, a Triple E class vessel carries 14.4 million boxes of trainers. If you've ever seen one of these monsters – in a port or on television – you will no doubt have been stunned by the sheer volume of the wall of containers rising up into the sky. But the most impressive part isn't even visible: there are just as many TEUs below deck, reaching well below the water line. Nor can you see that deep in their holds these ships have massive tanks containing more than 10,000 tonnes of diesel fuel. Doubling the size of the vessel cuts the cost of transporting a container by one-third. The companies operating the biggest vessels are more competitive and gain market share from others with fleets of smaller ships.

A whole series of additional systems are required to track movement. To accommodate mega-container ships, ports must extend their quays and dredge deeper basins; cranes must be taller, tractors faster, channels wider and so on. All this infrastructure must be supervised by states, which in turn eagerly subsidize it to boost trade and support the local economy. It is quite possible that the hidden costs of ancillary equipment, borne by the taxpayer, may exceed the economies of scale achieved by shipping companies. Were this the case, the race to build the biggest ever boat would actually damage the economy as a whole, artificially inflating the volume of trade and hence globalization.[1]

Slower Container Ships

An average vessel, steaming at 22 knots, burns about 100 tonnes of bunker fuel per day. Fuel represents by far the largest expenditure, up to 70% of the total cost of transport by container ship. In the late 2000s, the combination of high crude oil prices and a drop in international trade, due to the financial crisis, prompted shipping companies to reduce the speed of their fleets. Container ships started cruising the oceans at about 15 knots, the same speed as sailing clippers. The gain in fuel consumption was more than proportional, but journeys took longer and payroll costs were higher, with each ship completing fewer round trips. However, with crude oil nudging $100 a barrel and hundreds of container ships at anchor all over the world, doing nothing, fuel savings outstripped the additional expenses.

With the slump in oil prices since 2014, container ships have picked up a few knots, but they will never travel as fast as they once did. The container shipping industry is plagued by over-capacity and steaming more slowly goes some way to remedying the problem. The slower ships travel the more vessels are needed to transport the same volume of goods per month or per annum. So fewer ships lie idle or are scrapped, particularly as steel prices are low. Freight rates have picked up slightly which is another benefit for slow-steaming ship owners. Yet this will only have a marginal effect, because the impact of reducing capacity by slowing ships is itself only marginal compared to the massive over-capacity still haunting maritime transport.

Speed is dropping but journeys are sometimes getting longer too. Sailing home, from Europe to China, generally empty, container ships now take the long route round the Cape of Good Hope, rather than through the Red Sea. It is 5,000 kilometres longer but they save the toll for the Suez Canal.

Good Cartels to Avoid Destructive Competition?

Over-capacity encourages firms to consolidate and form alliances. After a few years of flat calm, takeovers are on the rise again. Let's look at two examples. CMA-CGM, based in Marseille, France, has purchased Singapore-registered Neptune Orient Lines. Meanwhile China's two largest carriers, Cosco and CSCL, have merged, forming the world's fourth largest container shipping company. Global alliances have also been established, much as in aviation. Such arrangements are about sharing of capacity and ships. In the first case a company reserves part – say 30% – of the capacity of ships operated by a partner operating the same route but at other dates. Co-operation of this sort delivers greater flexibility at a lower cost. In the second case members of an alliance pool some of their ships to serve a particular route. Here co-operation is designed to optimize capacity and frequency of service.

Such alliances are a throwback to the days of shipping conferences, which governed the life of regular lines for almost a century and a half. Ship owners gathered, often several times a year, to co-ordinate their choice of routes and sailing frequency. They often sought to manage capacity too. Unlike today's alliances, conference members also agreed on prices. For this reason competition regulators gradually banned such arrangements in the 1990s. After all, a system that allows competitors to fix the price of their goods, or in this case services, does look awfully like a cartel.

Underlining the unjustifiable nature of cartels, a form of monopoly with several players, a famous University of Chicago economist George J. Stigler, went so far as to describe it as industrial incest.[2] In common with many of his fellow economists he thought that an agreement between competitors on price or quantity was always a bad thing. However a few believe that it may, albeit rarely, have a certain merit.[3] Several have developed this idea in defence of shipping conferences: in some circumstances competition, they argue, can be destructive, particularly in the case of indivisible investment and perishable goods.[4] Both factors are present in line shipping: it is impossible to charter a tenth or a fifth of a ship to suit demand on a particular route. Similarly, even if hundreds of cubic metres of hold-space are empty, the ship must sail on time. This being the case, if demand for moving freight from port A to port B is not a multiple of the number of fully loaded vessels, competition leads to chaos. Some of the customers may be tempted to join forces to fill ships, forcing their competitors to pay more to ship the residual volume. For its part, a carrier may be tempted to delay departure and wait to fill up its hold, thus diverting part of the cargo destined for the following ship.

A Tale of Two Taxis

The 'taxi-trip game' may help to understand this particular situation.[5] Two cabs waiting outside an airport can carry, for a $5 fare equal to, two passengers at the most, each deriving a satisfaction equal to $10. If four passengers turn up, there is no problem: forming pairs, they share cabs and split the fare as they wish, earning together $15, or (2 x 10) – 5 per cab. On the other hand stable equilibrium is impossible if there are three passengers. Let's suppose they're called Tom, Dick and Harry. Tom and Dick team up and hail a taxi, each paying 2.5. At this juncture Harry may tap on Tom's window and offer to up the odds, paying $1 more: Harry will pay $3.5, instead of $5 if he travels on his own (10 – 5), and Tom $1.5 instead of $2.5. Dick, who is left standing in the road, finds himself in the same position as Harry, before, and may in turn raise the bidding to oust Tom. And so on it goes on.

Through a game with three simple non-equations we can show that a coalition between three passengers cannot be stable. In the first equation, each passenger must gain at least $5 to join a coalition, equivalent to what they would gain if they made the trip on their own. In the second non-equation each pair of passengers must gain at least $15, equivalent to what they would gain if they made the trip together ([2 x 10] – 5). In the third instance the coalition's maximum gain cannot exceed $20 ([3 x 10] – 10). There is no solution to this system. (The second non-equation means that the three pairs, or the equivalent of two triplets, must gain at least $45 [3 x 15], whereas the third one means that the three pairs cannot gain more than $40 [2 x 20]. QED). In other words, the competitive market is incapable of efficiently allocating three passengers to the two cabs on the rank outside the airport.

Of course if the three passengers were friends they could agree each to pay the same amount, in other words $3.33 (10 / 3) or one-third of the cost of two trips. Otherwise they might lose a friend. We might also imagine that a social norm requires each passenger to pay their fair share, proportional to their income, for instance. However the market does not provide collusive solutions of this sort: other institutions are needed. The same is true of shipping conferences which remedy the market's inability to achieve equilibrium.

Coalition and Conferences

This tempting argument is based on the branch of economic theory that studies the formation of coalitions: it is known as 'core' theory and was framed by Lester G. Telser, a most original economist also from University of Chicago.[6] However it is still a moot point whether it holds true for line shipping.[7] Drawing on data restricted to a few geographical areas and historical periods, econometric research has shown that the existence of conferences results in more traffic, which suggests they are efficient, invalidating in turn allegations they constitute a cartel: much as a monopoly, a cartel inevitably goes hand-in-hand with a drop in output.[8]

It would nevertheless be a mistake to generalize on the basis of this result. Conferences produce two contradictory outcomes, one in the general interest, the other not. By reaching agreement, shipping companies can remedy the lack of balance in a competitive market, much as the three passengers confronted by two cabs. That is the up side. They can negotiate prices or share out the market – in short, set up a cartel. That's the down side. In *The Wealth of Nations*, published in 1776, Adam Smith wrote: 'People of the same trade seldom meet together, even for merriment and diversion, but the conversation ends in a conspiracy against the public, or in some contrivance to raise prices.' The relative weight of the two outcomes, and hence their overall result, depends on the details of how a conference is organized and on demand. They can only be analysed one at a time.

To keep your economic bearings, just remember that joint action on prices by competing firms isn't always 'incestuous' but there is every reason to suspect a cartel. In economics, sailing by dead reckoning is the safest means of reaching your destination.

Notes

1. Merk, O. 'Maritime transport: too cheap to be good', *Shipping Today*, 8 April 2016.
2. Stigler, G. (1983), 'The economists and the problem of monopoly', *University of Chicago Law Occasional Paper*, 19.
3. Telser, L. (1988), *Theories of Competition*, Amsterdam: North-Holland.
4. Seidman, D. and Sheppard, E. (2001), 'Ocean shipping alliances: the wave of the future?', *International Journal of Maritime Economics*, 3: 351–367.
5. Bittlingmayer, G. (1989), 'The economic problem of fixed costs and what legal research can contribute', *Law and Social Inquiry*, 14: 739–762.
6. https://en.wikipedia.org/wiki/Lester_G._Telser
7. Competition issues in liner shipping, OECD working party 2 on competition XE 'competition' and regulation, memorandum for the 59th meeting, 19 June 2015.
8. Sjostrom, W. (1989), 'Collusion in ocean shipping: a test of monopoly and empty core models', *Journal of Political Economy*, 97: 1160–1179.

SIX

Intermezzo

The Earth Is Not That Flat

Drawing on a wide range of examples, we have seen that the notions of competition and market are closely linked. This has two consequences. The first prompts us to define competition in terms of a market's structural characteristics, such as the concentration of producers. The second puts the priority on market enlargement in order to understand changes in competition, in particular its extension through reductions in the cost of transport, which shrink distances. (We shall look at extension through product innovation – launching products that replace existing goods – in the third part of the book.)

Monopoly, perfect competition and oligopoly have come to be used in common parlance. A firm with a monopoly is the only agent supplying a market comprising numerous buyers; perfect competition describes a market in which a very large number of suppliers cater for a very large number of buyers; whereas in an oligopoly there are only a few suppliers. These basic concepts also pay great attention to the number of market agents, or, stated differently, the greater or lesser concentration of supply and demand. The same principle underpins two less commonly used terms: monopsony, a single vendor dealing with several buyers; and bilateral monopoly, a single vendor dealing with a single buyer.

The simple, intuitive idea is that the more a market is concentrated in just a few hands, the less competition there is. But the number of protagonists is obviously not the only factor determining the intensity of competition. Other variables are also at work, such as how well informed consumers are regarding prices – very low in the case of punters playing the slots, but very high for firms purchasing containers – or product quality, very poor for a pair of skis, until you've tried them on the slopes, nigh on perfect for operators purchasing natural gas. However, even taking into account these other structural factors, the same reasoning prevails: competition can be deduced from the characteristics of a market. Competition and market structure blend into one.

Testing Competition Theory Against Real Life

A second simple, intuitive idea belonging to the conventional approach is that competition is beneficial to consumers. The stiffer the competition, the less mark-up manufacturers can apply, which means lower prices and greater customer satisfaction. In technical terms, this means that in a market with perfect competition, price equals marginal cost, companies make no profit and consumer satisfaction, or surplus, is optimal.

We illustrated this approach in the first part with various straightforward case studies. The twenty-foot container market in the 1980s is an example of perfect competition, ski schools (in the United States) an instance of a monopolistic market, ski manufacturers and container shipping lines an oligopolistic market. With gas we have also seen the case of a bilateral monopoly, and with casinos a whole range of situations depending on their location.

But neither real life nor economic theory are quite that simple. The maritime transport industry is an oligopoly, yet it has seen periods of extremely intense competition; conversely competition has at times been weak in the container industry, which should in theory be perfectly competitive. Furthermore competition does not necessarily benefit consumers, indeed it may even be unfavourable to them. For instance it is better for skiers that the lifts at their favourite resort be operated by a monopoly, and that competition between a top ski manufacturer and a top binding manufacturer should be eliminated. Even a cartel of shipping lines can be beneficial for firms exporting goods.

So a measure of caution is required when dealing these two simple, intuitive ideas underpinning a structural approach to competition. They are only plausible, often right but sometimes wrong. It would be wiser just to treat them as a starting point for reasoning; take them to be right or wrong in the industry and market you're observing and try to check this assumption by studying the characteristics of the market and of competition.

Market Extension

A key merit of an approach closely linking competition and market is that it focuses on territory and borders. Markets have a geographical dimension that for obvious reasons must feature in any analysis of competition: the cost of transporting goods. Companies some distance apart cannot serve exactly the same customer base, nor can the latter play on rivalry between them. In the case of casinos, customers must actually travel there and consume on the spot. Much as for supermarkets, consumers pay the cost of transport directly, travelling by car or occasionally on foot. Manufacturing firms must deliver their goods. Take two, equally efficient companies: when serving a particular customer one will be penalized by the extra cost of logistics due to being at a different location. So competition between the two companies cannot be perfect.

From this point of view no product is wholly interchangeable, or in economic parlance perfectly substitutable. At first sight there is nothing that more closely resembles a twenty-foot container than another twenty-foot container. So there is no point in a customer choosing one manufacturer rather than another; all that matters is the price. But in practice price reflects cost. For a manufacturer based several thousand kilometres away the cost of delivery to the customer will be higher than for a manufacturer nearby. A Chinese container manufacturer must have a factory in Europe to deliver its goods there. The cost of shipping a brand-new container empty over long distances is prohibitive. Over and above the cost of transport itself, transaction costs may reduce the size of the market, and consequently the number of players, and hence in all likelihood the competition. Obtaining local information, contracting expenses, administrative formalities, customs clearance and so on are all invisible borders that act like taxes, raising barriers to market entry. In the chapters on Apple and Google we shall see how smartphone technology has contributed to reducing such transaction costs and driven a wave of digital globalization. But for the time being we shall restrict ourselves to globalizing trade, its causes and its effects on competition.

Two figures sum up the topic. Since the beginning of the 1970s international trade has increased three times faster than global output. Three-quarters of this increase has concerned countries that do not have a common border and most of the goods have travelled by sea, to a lesser extent by air.[1] The share of global trade travelling long distances is rising; the geographical extension of markets is consequently increasing.

It would however be a mistake to overplay this trend. Market integration is only partial and even now it would be more accurate to speak of semi-globalization. World trade accounts for less than a third of global output. Before the financial crisis it peaked at 29%. The extent to which markets have been internationalized, regardless of how it is measured, amounts to several tens of percentage points, certainly nothing verging on 100%. For example only 18% of US companies export and these exports only account for 15% of all the goods they despatch. Of the companies that do sell their goods abroad, 64% only export to one country, compared to a mere 14% selling to five or more countries.[2] We are a very long way from a situation in which all the companies on Earth cater for all the consumers. In short, distance is not dead and the world is nothing like as flat as suggested by the title of a popular book on globalization.[3]

All the markets do not encompass the globe, but it is likely that almost all of them have extended their reach since the 1970s – perhaps by a few dozen kilometres for local markets, possibly by several hundred kilometres for regional markets, by several thousand kilometres for continental markets. No data is available to measure such extension, but growth along these lines is plausible, because the cost of road transport over short and medium distances has fallen and consumer mobility increased. Consider, as a minor instance, the fact that the choice of a ski resort was once restricted to a nearby valley or massif but now embraces a much larger number of possible venues, some overseas. Top resorts in the French, Austrian and Swiss Alps now compete directly. The generalized geographical extension of markets, even the smallest ones, is what interests us here, because it entails, all other things being equal, more intense competition.

The Causes of Enlargement

Let's take a closer look at the two main reasons for market extension: opening of borders and liberalization of economies, coupled with lower transport costs.

The end of the Cold War put a stop to once watertight barriers to trade. It also delivered a 'peace dividend', enabling cuts in military spending, and greater investment in other sectors and beyond national borders.[4] Furthermore the pressure of customs duty and non-tariff barriers was reduced almost everywhere. Liberalizing trade became a political priority for many countries. To this was added more specifically local or national liberalization of network industries, opening up to competition whole swathes of industry, from telecommunications to air transport, through electricity and gas. Finally a whole series of developing countries undertook economic reforms and set about catching up with the western countries which played a leading role in international trade. In 1980, South Korea, India and Thailand were not among the top developing countries for exports. China clung to tenth place in this ranking. It has since taken the lead, but also in all categories of global exporters, be they developed, emerging or not. Chinese companies now feature in international rankings based on revenue. One-fifth of the world's 500 largest companies are registered in China, and three of them are in the top ten.

But China would not have become the workshop of the world without the phenomenal drop in transport costs. Its containers loaded with goods now irrigate the whole planet, filled with toys, smartphones and even skis. The cost of freight has been halved since the 1970s.[5] The invention of the container, aka the big box, has revolutionized transport and the associated logistics with specially designed ships, port infrastructure and land facilities. It has been one of the main factors in slashing the cost per tonne-kilometre of moving goods, not so much because it has lowered the basic cost of shipping by sea or air, but rather because it has cut the total cost of door-to-door transport by facilitating loading and unloading at switches from one mode to another. After all the goods in containers are not consumed in the immediate vicinity of ports or airports! Between their point of departure and arrival goods are carried by lorries some of the time, and road transport itself has become cheaper. For example in France its cost was cut by a third between 1978 and 1998, despite payroll expenditure rising over the same period. The main causes here were deregulation and a fall in the price of heavy goods vehicles. Meanwhile the drop in the cost of air transport has been spectacular, far greater than for maritime shipping. Its growth rate has been equally impressive, demand for swift delivery having increased. It takes about five weeks for a ship to travel from Asia to Europe, compared to 24 hours, or maybe less, for a plane to reach almost any other airport in the world. Air freight is the only solution for most perishable goods, but it is also increasingly used for goods that are not: restocking garments that consumers have liked; new models of premium smartphones shipped to shops as soon as they are produced for sale to aficionados. It is also the fall in the cost of passenger air transportation that has extended the mass-tourism market. Las Vegas and Macao no longer only attract a regional clientele, eager to have a flutter and maybe lose their shirt.

In the first part we have seen how competition is connected to a geographical market. But over and above territory, a market is defined by the characteristics of the product traded there. These are the features that can make an object specific, even unique, or alternatively one that can easily be substituted by similar goods. In the following part we shall look at this other dimension.

Notes

1. Ghemawat, P. (2010), 'The globalization of markets', in Globalization notes series, IESE insights.
2. Bernard, A., Jensen, B., Redding, S. and Schott, P. (2007), 'Firms in international trade', *Journal of Economic Perspectives*, 21: 105–130.
3. Cairncross, F. (2001), *The Death of Distance: How the Communications Revolution Is Changing Our Lives*, Boston, MA: Harvard Business School Press; Friedman, T. (2007), *The World Is Flat: a Brief History of the Twenty-First Century*, New York, NY: Farrar, Straus and Giroux.
4. *World Trade Report 2013: Factors Determining the Future of World Trade*, World Trade Organization.
5. Hummels, D. (2009), 'Globalization and freight transport costs in maritime shipping and aviation', International Transport Forum, Paris.

PART II

Competition and Differentiation

The general principle of free choice in the spending of one's income includes not only freedom to vary the proportions between the larger categories of food, shelter, etc., but freedom also to express a market demand for Smith's sausages if one believes them superior to Jones's.

E. H. Chamberlin, *Monopoly and Competition*, 1954

This part looks at products targeting the final consumer, people like you and me. The particularity of such goods is immediately apparent: they are available in a huge range of variants. Just look at the shelves of your local supermarket: there isn't just one cola-flavoured soda, but at least four or five different sorts; similarly there isn't just one breakfast cereal, more like a dozen or so, not one wine but at least twenty; and so it goes on. Apart from a few basic goods such as bananas or salt (maybe not even this staple) it is now hard to find a product of which only one specimen is on sale. They all differ by at least one characteristic such as brand, size, packaging, source or composition. As western consumers we live in a world of massive differentiation. And that changes everything when it comes to competition . . .

SEVEN

Coca-Cola Versus Pepsi

The War Is Over

The intake of cola-flavoured sodas is falling off. In the United States consumption of Coca-Cola has dropped to just under 100 litres per person per year. Which is still quite a lot. Sales of Pepsi-Cola are not faring any better. Consumers in the developed world are gradually giving up sodas, and the battle against overweight is now a public-health priority. As a modest contribution to combating this scourge, I should point out that a 33 centilitre can of Coke or Pepsi contains 38 grams of sugar, equivalent to nine teaspoons. If you were to drink six litres a day, like Kathy O'Sullivan, a young mother of two, your daily sugar intake would exceed half a kilo.[1]

So does the decline of soda consumption herald a truce between the two cola giants? Why carry on fighting when your customers are deserting you, not for a competitor but for healthier beverages?

Duel or Duopoly

But was there ever actually a war? It is surely high time to debunk this misleading representation of competition as a zero-sum game, or worse still a negative-sum game. When, as is the case here, it involves two competitors, it is wrongly presented as a sort of boxing match.

This sort of conception suggests that competition is only destructive. One of the two protagonists must disappear, eliminated by a knock-out blow. The fist-fight inevitably ends with a winner and a loser. It's a zero-sum game. The martial metaphor is even more misguided because war destroys much more wealth than it creates. Competition can certainly be violent and companies aggressive, but it is a positive-sum game. For an economist, competition is the key incentive driving business to cut costs and innovate. As a result consumers have the benefit of cheaper, better quality goods and services. For business itself the gain may be far from negligible because lower prices and innovation stimulate demand.

In other words, if we see competition as a combat sport, we're only getting a snapshot which wholly overlooks consumers. Sure enough when the Coca-Cola Company lowers its prices, it wins customers from its rival. It's the same when PepsiCo hires Michael Jackson for an advertising campaign. For the firms it is indeed a zero or negative-sum game when the competition adopts the same strategy of lower prices or publicity spending. But this is only true if we take a static view.

You may think it's going a bit far to suggest a positive, dynamic vision of competition with regard to cola-flavoured sodas, given that competition boosts demand for a product not necessarily too good for health. Economic theory would say that if the behaviour of consumers is prejudicial to third-parties or society – for example because obesity is hard on the public purse – it is up to government to take the appropriate measures. Which is beginning to happen. The governments of Indiana, Chicago, Mexico, France and even the island of Saint Helena, among others, have introduced tax on sodas. If the competition heats up in polluting industries or the market for cocaine, the solution is not to rein it in order to reduce production but to act on prices through taxation or make it an offence.

Rivalry between Coca-Cola and PepsiCo is not a form of warfare: it is a competitive oligopoly. We might even say it's a duopoly because the two firms control almost the entire market for soda-flavoured colas. But with demand falling in developed countries, competition is slackening and its focus shifting. Let's take a more detailed look at all this.

Competition Between Substitutable Goods

Duopolistic competition in the cola market does not impact so much on price as on other dimensions. Yet there is surely nothing more like a can of Coke than a can of Pepsi? However, in a duopoly based on perfectly substitutable goods, competition impacts solely on price and annihilates any hope of profit for either firm. Just over a century ago, the French mathematician Joseph Bertrand demonstrated that in such a case a duopoly's equilibrium price is equal to the marginal cost, the same price as in a situation of perfect competition with a very large number of producers! If one of the two firms sets a price slightly lower than its competitor, all the consumers in the market will buy the former's product; the second firm must in turn set an even lower price to corner the market. This process of successive price cuts will end when the price can go no lower, in other words when it equals the unit cost. Below that limit the company would lose money. Obviously the lack of any constraint on the production capacity of the two players is a key assumption in this model. And of course it does not hold true for Coca-Cola and Pepsi. Gigantic as it is, their individual capacity for manufacturing cola concentrate and bottling soda does not match total demand.

But in any case, cut-throat competition of this sort does not apply to our duopoly because their products are not perfectly substitutable, due to the corresponding brands. The findings of laboratory tests are categorical. Subjected to blind tests consumers are unable to say whether the beverage they have tasted is Coke or Pepsi. The proportion of right answers does not significantly differ from the results of random choice. The results are the same when the glasses presented and tasted one after another contain different colas, or contain the same beverage, but without test participants being told they are drinking the same thing each time. Regarding their preferences, it seems that Pepsi came out on top in the blind tests. But this result is disputed, as it is based mainly on tests organized by Pepsi in supermarkets. Critics claim that its cola was served slightly cooler than the rival beverage, which biased the outcome. An alternative explanation, slightly less machiavellian, is that Pepsi has a slightly higher sugar content. Both the palate and the brain of homo sapiens like the taste of sugar.

Either way, consumer preferences change with any mention of brands. Witness real-life experience: shoppers buy more Coke than Pepsi in supermarkets, where the two brands appear side by side. Magnetic-resonance imagery confirms this advantage. An experiment reported in a neuroscience journal showed that the same part of the brain was activated when a participant in a blind test drank Coke or Pepsi.[2] In contrast, when they knew it was Coke another part of the brain lit up too, revealing a particular emotion. So clearly brand awareness leaves its mark on our minds! Their preference for Coke is probably due to advertising. The Atlanta-based firm spends more than \$2 billion a year on publicity, far outstripping Pepsi. It has been doing so for decades.

Price, Switching Costs and Other Tools

With regard to competition, the presence of brands creates friction in demand, which economists refer to as switching costs. Such friction is equal to the sum that must be given to a consumer for them to accept a change of product or supplier. According to recent research, consumers of Coke would switch to the competitor's cola on condition they were given 30 cents a can, which would be equivalent to selling Pepsi with a 30% discount on its current price.[3] Just 13 cents would convince adepts of Pepsi to switch brands. However one cannot generalize on the basis of these figures. The relevant research was based exclusively on purchasing behaviour in a supermarket of a large US city in the early 1990s. It does nevertheless illustrate that Coke drinkers display greater loyalty to their preferred brand than their Pepsi fellows. This no doubt explains why Coke is on sale almost everywhere and always more expensive than Pepsi.

So Coca-Cola and Pepsi do not compete on price, apart from promotional drives linked in particular to moving into a new area or launching new packaging. Moreover, there have been few periods of price war. Competition is nevertheless very real: it just takes other forms. Let's look at three examples.

First, competition in publicity to create and maintain brand loyalty, and consequently recruit stars too. Sticking with the duel theme, Olympic boxer Marlen Esparza punches for Coke, whereas amateur wrestler Henry Cejudo fights for Pepsi.

Second, competition for control of upstream activities in order to contain costs and prices. For a long time, an independent network was tasked with processing concentrate, bottling – now mainly canning – and distribution. Thanks to a series of acquisitions, Coca-Cola and PepsiCo have gradually taken over these companies. In the USA, this was a massive undertaking, leaving independent bottling plants with less than 15% market share.[4]

Third, competition for the exclusive presence of their goods to capture more customers, and to trigger and secure loyalty. On supermarket shelves the duopoly's products are stacked side by side, often competing with other brands, such as Sam's Cola at Walmart or Cola Classic at Carrefour. In contrast, consumers have no choice at filling stations, cafeterias, snack bars or even baker's shops. In this sort of outlet, space is too limited to install several refrigerated cabinets stocked with bottles and cans. There is keen rivalry between Coca-Cola and PepsiCo to reach exclusive agreements with such retailers, for it is a way of generating repeat sales. Part of the customer base of such outlets are regulars. The chances are that when they go elsewhere they will purchase the cola that has, by force of habit, become their preferred choice. Competition between the brands is even stiffer to obtain exclusive contracts with leading chains and keep the soda fountain flowing. McDonald's is Coca-Cola's top blue-chip customer. The Atlanta-based brand also has an exclusive contract with Burger King. If you prefer Tex-Mex food, chicken rather burgers, you'll be drinking Pepsi at Taco Bell or KFC.

Innovation and Its Limits

Lastly, competition is a key driving force for innovation. The world of Coca Light, Pepsi Light, Coca-Cola Zero, Pepsi Max, Coke Life and Next Pepsi has not always existed. PepsiCo started the ball rolling with artificial sweeteners replacing saccharine. That was in 1964. Veteran consumers will no doubt recall the stunning flop of New Coke. This new recipe with a slightly sweeter taste was rolled out in 1985 to coincide with the brand's hundredth anniversary. The plan was for it to completely replace the previous version, blind tests having shown that a majority of participants preferred it to Pepsi Cola and conventional Coke.

The switch was announced on 23 April, with production of the traditional recipe stopping a week later. But as there is a chasm between what people prefer during blind tests and in real life, many consumers started hoarding the old stuff and thousands of others indignantly complained to the firm by phone or in writing. Word has it that even Fidel Castro, a great Coke drinker, joined the uprising. He purportedly saw the change as yet another sign of the decadence of capitalism.

Coca-Cola reacted by relaunching the traditional beverage three months later. Classic and New Coke co-existed for a few years, then the newcomer vanished into the dustbin of history and Classic became good old Coke again. The year of the Coca-Cola centenary was one of the rare occasions when Pepsi sales exceed those of Coke.

Less Intense Competition

In the world of today, with the steady slide in demand for sodas, competition is less intense. Indeed, we are seeing the opposite of a price war. If Coca-Cola ups its price, Pepsi follows suit, and vice-versa. But there is nothing co-ordinated about this process, no collusion akin to what we have seen in cartels or alliances (see Chapter 5). With falling demand becoming a durable trend there is less pressure to make dynamic price trade-offs. The choice between reaping the benefits of brand loyalty today by selling at a higher price to loyal customers, or broadening the future customer base by setting a lower price to poach the competition's consumers has shifted.

The focus of competition has also moved as demand has declined. Coca-Cola and PepsiCo do not only market cola-flavoured water containing varying amounts of sugar, they also sell mineral water, fruit juice, smoothies and such. PepsiCo has taken the lead here, doing much more to diversify into other beverages. It is investing more in health-conscious drinks than the Atlanta firm and has done for longer. But the war – which is not a war – is still being waged on the original battlefield – which is not a battlefield either – for there is still much to be done to slake the thirst for cola among the middle classes of India, China and other Asian countries.

Notes

1. *Daily Mail*, 24 January 2016, www.dailymail.co.uk/femail/article-3414263/Mum-addicted-Coke-drinks-SIX-LITRES.html.
2. McClure, S. et al. (2004), 'Neural correlates of behavioral preference for culturally familiar drinks', *Neuron*, 44: 379–387.
3. Chan, T., Cosguner, K. and Seetharaman, S. (2012), 'Structural econometric model of dynamic manufacturer pricing: a case study of the cola market', Social Science Research Network.
4. Slind, M. and Yoffie, D. (2006), 'Cola wars continue: Coke and Pepsi in 2006', *Harvard Business School Case 706–447*.

EIGHT

A Cruise in a Gilded Cage

Surely at some time or another every company has dreamt of captive customers, sure to consume its goods, all its goods and nothing but its goods. Cruise operators seem to have found the right answer, putting their customers on a ship and sailing the seas for seven days at a stretch.

Cruise ships have become floating Club Meds, tourist complexes and destinations in their own right.[1] They provide passengers with bed and board, as well as all sorts of recreational activities such as a water park, practice golf course, ice-skating rink, climbing wall, spa, planetarium, night club, casino, bar, library, tropical garden and tattoo saloon, not to mention attractions for the kids and no end of boutiques. With so many amenities, excursions almost take second place. *Oasis of the Sea*, sporting 2,700 cabins spread over 18 decks, offers all of the above and more besides. And as its name suggests, it is just as attractive a destination for cruise-lovers as its Caribbean ports of call.

A Captive Market . . . That Floats

Entertainment onboard may be free of charge, or not. That is to say, included in the price of the ticket, or not. Passengers may indulge in free activities as much as they like, without dipping in their pocket. Typically there is no charge for swimming pools and sports facilities. But there are supplements for gaming, bars, beauticians and of course perfume, jewellery and souvenirs. In terms of a cruise company's revenue, the average breakdown is 70% for tickets and the rest for supplements. In contrast, sales of tickets have a negligible impact on profit,[2] supplements making up the lion's share.[3] The challenge for operators is to attract customers by building beautiful gilded cages, lure them aboard with finely targeted prices, then offer them the paying services they like. Lets look at how they achieve this, while noting that competition is still very lively in this business.

Cruise ships grow steadily bigger and more splendid, in other words better equipped. *Harmony of the Sea*, launched in 2016, is 362 metres long, displaces approximately 120,000 tonnes and can carry 6,360 passengers. She is marginally bigger than her sister ships. Novelties include the world's largest dry slides, a bionic bar and themed entertainment by Dreamworks. Built by the STX shipyard in Saint-Nazaire, France, this vessel cost $1.35 billion.

Bigger and Bigger

Twenty years ago, cabins didn't have balconies, nor were there spas, skating rinks and climbing walls; liners were half the size. Pressure to build bigger ships with more attractions is linked to economies of scale and competition. But the notion of economies of scale here does not mean the vessel must be larger to contain bigger swimming pools, longer slides or more tennis courts. On the contrary it refers to the advantage derived from cutting unit costs through greater capacity: in the present instance, a lower cost per berth thanks to a larger number of berths on each ship, and more broadly a lower passenger-day cost thanks to increased tonnage.

With bigger, more attractive ships, operators can deliver more affordable cruises and greater value for money, thus appealing to a wider clientele. This gives them a competitive advantage over other cruise companies, but also over sectors of the travel trade.

As a product, cruises are easily interchangeable. They are competing with holidays on dry land: a tourist complex on an island in the Bahamas; a theme park at Orlando, Florida; or a hotel and casino on the Strip at Las Vegas. In recent years the cruise industry has succeeded in increasing its market share compared to such competition, which explains its very high growth, averaging 7% since the early 1980s. Its customer base also reflects this trend, with cruises becoming a mass-consumption product. What do you think is the average age of cruise-lovers? Sixty-five? Not at all, though that was the case in 1995. It has now dropped to 49.[4]

The Beauties of Yield Management

However, once you've built a big boat you need to fill it! It's not enough to have a beautiful gilded cage to pull in the cruisers. You must sell them berths. But how? Through yield management, a technique for managing unit revenue by variable targeted prices. It is now standard practice in businesses with fixed costs and time-limited products, such as tickets, to use this technique to set prices. Cruise operators share both characteristics with other branches of the hospitality industry. Much as for hotels or theme parks, the occupancy rate of amenities is the key determinant for profits. Even if all the tickets haven't been sold, the boat must sail. As a result, earnings may not cover the cost of fuel and onboard staff, which is the same regardless of the number of passengers, less still pay off the cost of the ship. Cruise reservations open 18 months before the date of sailing. During this period prices will vary depending on cabin occupancy, falling if demand is lower than expected, or on the contrary rising. Yield management here is particularly sophisticated because, unlike a train or plane, for a cruise liner the system must keep track of much more than just a limited range of seats and classes, juggling with variables such as the occupancy of staterooms, in various shapes and sizes, cabins with a view of the sea or deck, with or without a balcony, of different sizes (14, 18 or 24 square metres), on an upper or lower deck, among others.

What Is the Real Price?

Managers setting base prices may pitch them very low, lower even than the variable cost per passenger, because of course they take into account revenue from the add-ons passengers purchase onboard. So there is a big incentive to sell tickets cheap because any loss on this share of revenue can be recouped through profits on add-ons. In the last analysis, if competition between cruise companies to lure passengers into their gilded cages was perfect, they would make no profit at all, simply compensating on the one hand what they lose on the other.

However in practice a whole range of factors reduce this risk, particularly, that some penny-pinching cruisers will be reluctant to pay for both tickets and add-ons.[5] An aggressive price to lure a customer away from the competition will attract too many thrifty passengers, and not enough big spenders, with high willingness to pay for both ticket and supplements. In short, pricing strategies can be a real headache, but one that cruise operators have definitely mastered, filling their liners with exceptionally high occupancy rates. By the time the ship sails almost all the cabins are taken. Moreover their profits are sufficiently high for them to place regular orders for more gigantic vessels.

Profit in Add-Ons

Once passengers are onboard, it is essential that they consume add-ons in a manner advantageous to the operator. But this doesn't mean they should be taken for a ride, because they'd never come back a second time! In practice, six out of ten cruise passengers give it a second try, often with the same company. Furthermore, although they can only spend their money onboard, they are at liberty to purchase fewer add-ons, or none at all. Add-ons are priced close to willingness to pay, which enables cruise companies to optimize the yield on the attractions they offer.

Outings at ports of call are a different matter, as operators have no way of capturing at least part of what passengers spend. They minimize revenue losses in various ways, such as setting up wholly owned subsidiaries to organize excursions for their passengers, or taking a cut on any purchases their customers make in souvenir shops or restaurants. Short of not stopping at all, the most radical solution is to develop your own port of call. MSC Croisières, for instance, has bought an idyllic island covering some 38 hectares. In so doing, it has copied other cruise companies operating in the Caribbean and Bahamas, which have had a base there for many years. MSC is in the process of building restaurants, bars and other amenities on its island, a dry-land extension to the gilded cage.

The cruise industry is certainly profitable but not as much as other sectors with such high market concentration (the top three cruise lines hold four-fifths of the world market), product differentiation and price discrimination. This is because competition is still keen.

First, thanks to competition between individual companies. In the short term, they compete with one another to fill their ships, particularly when the overall economic climate is gloomy. In the long term, they are vying to boost capacity, by building the biggest, most attractive new vessels. There are few specialist ship-yards and they are open to all comers. The game is open to everyone, even small operators focusing on niche markets but out to grow, or new entrants from Asia.

Second, due to competition from other sectors of the travel trade. Raising the average price of a cruise is risky because consumers may take their custom elsewhere. The price elasticity of demand is high, about −2.0. So a 10% hike in prices would lead to a 20% drop in ticket sales.[6]

It's time to book next summer's Mediterranean cruise. Prices are low, so go for it, but bear in mind that if you are tempted by lots of add-ons it will certainly cost you more than expected. But who cares! Better to make the most of a few days in a gilded cage.

Notes

1. Dehoorne, O. and Petit-Charles, N. (2011), 'Tourisme de croisière et industrie de la croisière', *Études caribéennes*.
2. Larsen, S. et al. (2013), 'Belly full, purse closed: cruise line passengers' expenditures', *Tourism Management Perspectives*, 6: 142–148.
3. Savioli, M. and Zirulia, L. (2015), 'Add-on pricing: theory and evidence from the cruise industry', *Quaderni* working paper DSE 1.
4. Sciozzi, D. et al. (2015), 'Structural analysis of cruise passenger traffic in the world and in the Republic of Croatia', *Scientific Journal of Maritime Research*, 29: 8–15.
5. Ellison, G. (2005), 'A model of add-on pricing', *Quarterly Journal of Economics*, 120: 585–637.
6. Lerner, A., Scheffman, D. and Simons, J. (2003), 'The FTC cruise line merger investigation', *Brown Bag Program*, ABA Section of Antitrust Law.

NINE

Lego's Winning Game

Lego Group is the world's largest toy company, leading a highly competitive industry in terms of both price and product variety. At Christmas each year we gaze at shop windows and catalogues, at a loss for choice even when we know the children who will be receiving the gifts. A construction kit or a football, a doll or a furry animal, a board or video game? A box of Duplo or Mega Bloks? A Barbie doll or a Disney Princess? Monopoly or Trivial Pursuit? What's more, we must keep an eye on the price, so as not to overrun our gift budget. Every toy manufacturer is fighting for a share of our spending. Let's construct, brick by Lego brick, the complex competitive game they are playing.

Demanding Toy Consumers

We shall start with market structure. Variations in the number and behaviour of children is a key component in the games economy. The number of children in the United States and the European Union is stable, but has dropped in Japan. These three entities account for two-thirds of the world toy market. With the fall in the number of children in China, due to the one-child policy, no miracles can be expected any time soon. In addition, childhood is growing shorter. Increasingly early on children are protesting that they are 'too old to be playing'. So with natural demand in decline, competition between manufacturers is inevitably growing.

Another key feature of this framework is that the end-users are very rarely the ones doing the buying. Adults only buy a few per cent of global production for their own use, but they pay for the rest too. Even at Lego there are not many people like David Beckham buying the Taj Mahal set (5,922 pieces, recommended retail price £199.99) for their own amusement. This means that the marketing and merchandizing policies of toy manufacturers must appeal to the eyes of children and the pockets of adults. Never an easy task. As any parent knows, our preferences do not necessarily coincide with those of our offspring.

Santa's Workshop in China

One figure sums up the production side of this market structure: 80% of all toys are manufactured in China.[1] Santa Claus is Chinese. As sales are extremely seasonal, there is little scope for business to adjust output in line with successful products. The logistics chain is inflexible because all but the most expensive toys travel by sea, not by air. Allow four to five weeks from Shanghai to Rotterdam.

Competition explains why production is located in Asia and the lower prices. Toy manufacturers started turning to China in the early 1990s in a bid to cut costs. Since then almost everyone has followed suit, bringing prices down, by 17% in France for instance, over the past 20 years.[2] This trend explains why the stack of toys under the Christmas tree has climbed higher every year and children's bedrooms have become increasingly cluttered.

Lego is an exception to this rule. Until 2000, all its bricks were Danish-made. Now they are also produced in Mexico and eastern Europe. Its first factory in China started production in November 2016 and will only be catering for the Asian market. As for the price of Lego bricks, it only started to drop significantly in the early 2000s when the firm was restructured. High overheads and ill-conceived diversification projects had brought the Danish firm to the verge of bankruptcy.

The last key feature of this market structure is the high concentration of distribution channels. There are many specialist toy shops – about 20,000 in Europe – but they only account for a tiny share of sales.[3] Big specialist firms such as Toys "R" Us or major retailers such as Walmart and Auchan, dominate the brick and mortar market. The picture is the same for online sales – currently a quarter of the total – led by Amazon and eBay.[4] In the face of such concentration, the toy industry itself looks fairly fragmented. The five largest players only account for about a third of the global market. In the USA, this share rises to 50% but the balance of power still favours mass distribution. Walmart, for example, handles about 40% of sales by the two largest US toy manufacturers, Hasbro and Mattel.

Growing Segmentation and Differentiation

So the structure of this market does little to facilitate high margins for toy firms. Fortunately, seen from the outside, the market seems to display growing segmentation and differentiation. With competition exerting pressure on a narrower segment, with less interchangeable goods, there is still some room for manoeuvre.

Let's look, for example, at gender-based distinctions in toys. In 1975 a well-known North American catalogue explicitly noted only 2% of toys as specifically targeting girls or boys. That figure now exceeds 50%.[5] These days it's a hard struggle to find a gender-neutral bicycle for a three- to five-year-old child. Thanks to this separation, competition between the two US giants is less direct. On the one hand, we have Hasbro with Action Man, GI Joe and a range of Star Wars figures; on the other, Mattel with Barbie, Kitchen Play and American Dolls.

Measured in relation to the market segment, concentration is much higher, giving less leverage to the bargaining power of mass retailers. Sales of Lego sets represent three-quarters of the market for construction toys; before her fall from favour Barbie accounted for half of all sales of dolls.

In the various market segments, the race to differentiate has moved on. Brands have taken onboard video and hi-tech content, adding them to a whole series of conventional features – colour, design, safety, etc. Toys reflect or tell a story, such as The Force Awakens or The Snow Queen. The toy industry has an insatiable appetite for licensing movie content, particularly from Disney. It's annual sales now depend on the release schedule of Hollywood blockbusters. But firms also produce their own content to boost sales. Hasbro's Transformer toys have become big-screen heroes in their own right. The Lego Movie, released in 2014, was a commercial success both as a film on general release and as a boxed set. Toys have become technological objects too, communicating with one another and the Internet. They exist in virtual form as applications for tablets and smartphones. Far from being just the opposite of something dull, a smart toy can learn from its owner's behaviour, the better to suit their needs.

A Matter of Positioning

To grasp the effects of segmentation and differentiation on competition, it's hard to outdo the tale of two ice-cream sellers.[6] The vendors must choose where to pitch their respective stalls on a beach along which potential customers are evenly spread. If they both aim for the middle, trading side by side, rivalry will be more intense but each one can capture the whole market. If, on the other hand, they move to either end, they will each have their own clientele to some extent, seaside holiday-makers being reluctant to walk too far for a cornet. This means fewer potential buyers but less competition too, so a higher unit mark-up. A good compromise might be to locate the stalls at a reasonable distance from each other, for example between the centre and either end of the beach.

Now, in the place of the beach, imagine a range of consumer preferences, with the degree of product differentiation instead of distance. This should help to understand the positioning of the various toy manufacturers with regard to differentiation. The only people in the middle ground are those touting counterfeit goods, copies of successful products at knocked down prices. Top firms, such as long-standing global leader Lego, are located at one extremity. On average, everyone on Earth possesses 102 Lego bricks. Next Christmas will add a couple more.

Till then, a word of advice to all kids: 'LEg GOdt' (play well in Danish).

Notes

1. Study on the competitiveness of the toy industry, European Competitiveness and Sustainable Industrial Policy consortium (ECSIP), 30 August 2013.
2. Consumer price index (monthly, all households, mainland France, baseline 1998), series 000638945, French National Institute of Statistics and Economic Studies (Insee).
3. Study on the competitiveness of the toy industry, ECSIP, ibid.
4. Muller, L. (2015), 'The western toy market,' *TD Monthly*.
5. Sweet, E. (2014), 'Toys are more divided by gender now than they were 50 years ago', *The Atlantic*.
6. https://en.wikipedia.org/wiki/Hotelling's law.

TEN

Breakfast Cereals Invading Space

What is the connection between Kellogg's Special K, Cheerios or Quaker Oats and space? None at all, if you're thinking of launching satellites and the diet of astronauts. On the other hand, as we're talking about competition it's all too obvious: breakfast-cereal brands are competing in several dimensions of space before reaching your morning bowl of goodies.

Every year, Americans buy 2.7 billion boxes of breakfast cereals. Stacked one on top of another they would reach to the Moon and back.[1] The British are the biggest consumers, in terms of the quantity they eat (not their body weight), in keeping with their traditional love of porridge. They crunch through almost 7 kilos a year per head.

Few Players, Many Products

The breakfast-cereal industry is a differentiated oligopoly, with few players but a very large number of different products. The top three firms, Kellogg's, General Mills and PepsiCo, make 63% of global sales in a market nudging $30 billion.[2]

This overall picture obviously glosses over considerable diversity. The inhabitants of English-speaking countries alone (6% of the world's population), consume 54% of the total volume. The three companies cited above, much as their closest competitors, are multi-brand, multi-product operations. For example the generic brand

Kashi belongs to Kellogg's, which also produces Honey Pops, Frosties, All Bran, among others.

Similarly, PepsiCo owns Quaker Oats, which makes Cap'n Crunch. If you decided to try a new variety every day it would take almost ten years to sample all of them. In terms of diversity of supply, the number of different breakfast cereals available in the United States is only exceeded by the myriad newspaper titles (over 5,000). To get another take on the enormous product range, check out Wikipedia's long list, stretching in alphabetical order from All Bran to Zany Fruits (with mouth-watering visuals as an added bonus!).

So how are we to explain such profusion (or indeed proliferation: only twenty-five varieties of ready-to-eat breakfast cereal were registered in 1950, rising to eighty in 1972[3])? The immediate answer is that consumers, who have very divergent tastes, demand variety. But it is also because a company can reduce the likelihood of competition from new entrants by launching a new variant.

Competition Exerts Its Pressure in Space

What, you may ask, has competition to do with space? To fully understand the previous question you must accept that competition operates in spatial terms. You can grasp this intuitively with regard to geographical space. Suppose you're walking up Seventh Avenue in New York City and you fancy a coffee, you can choose between dozens of places. Your choice will depend on where you are, and where they are. If you favour Starbucks you will have to decide between going the extra distance to the next outlet, and stopping at Hard Rock Café, which is closer but less to your liking.

Product space is actually just the same. Let's see how. The simplest approach is to restrict ourselves to a one-dimensional space. Suppose that from the consumer's point of view breakfast cereals only differ by sugar content. The different varieties are positioned along a straight-line segment, comparable to Seventh Avenue, ranging from the least sweet to the sweetest, moving up from the south of Manhattan. In the present case, however, consumers are positioned according to their preference for sugar. In the absence of data showing that there is a proportionately higher number of consumers who prefer a specific sugar content, we shall assume that they are evenly distributed all the way along the line segment. Continuing our analogy, it is as if at any point in time there were an equal number of pedestrians all the way up Seventh Avenue. Equivalent to the distance to your preferred coffee shop is the loss of consumer satisfaction on choosing a breakfast cereal that contains either too little or too much sugar.

Let us now suppose that two characteristics – sugar content and crunchiness – distinguish the cereals. The varieties will now be positioned in a two-dimensional space, as in the figure below.

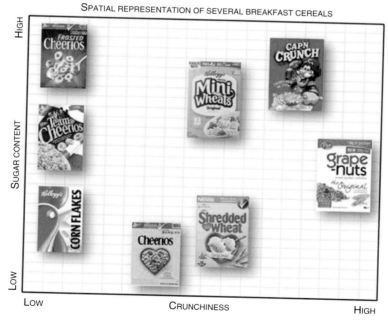

Figure 10.1: Spatial representation of several breakfast cereals

The consumers themselves do not feature on the chart because, as above, we have assumed they are not subject to any particular trend and are consequently evenly spread all over the square. If we wanted to show a specific trend, such as a large proportion of consumers liking sugar and crunch, all we would need to do is add a point cloud in the top right-hand corner. In this case demand for Cap'n Crunch would be greater than for Frosted Cheerios or Grape Nuts. Always supposing the price is the same, of course. Otherwise some consumers would be prepared to override their preferences and choose a cheaper cereal, at some distance from their ideal.

Spatial Location and Corporate Strategy

In practice, consumers are interested in many other aspects of breakfast cereals, such as the size of grains or the dry fruit, chocolate, protein or fibre content. Supposing there are ten characteristics each variety would need to be positioned in a ten-dimensional space. The same would apply to consumers! Of course this is impossible to represent on a chart and we would have to resort to mathematical notation, which I shall spare you.

However the spatial location of products and consumers does make it possible to study competition and corporate strategy.[4] Let's look at two limit, or extreme, cases that are among the most straightforward. If all consumers have the same taste they will prefer the same variety. Only this variety will be on the market and businesses will compete solely on price. Competition will focus on a single point in space, surrounded by a complete vacuum. In a second limit case, if it costs no less to produce two identical packets of cereal than two different packets, the market will reflect the ideal variety for each consumer. So you can see that a balance needs to be found between product differentiation and economies of scale. The further you pursue one goal, the less benefit you will derive from the other, leading to high costs and prices. Which means that for a given set of consumer preferences and production-cost functions, there is an economically optimal number of varieties on offer. It is in general greater than one, it being rare for consumer tastes not to differ, even slightly, and less than several tens of thousands because production requires a minimum amount of fixed investment at the outset.

For a firm, this particular form of 'space race' entails choosing the right spot to locate its product. Let's go back to our one-dimensional example, with a line segment running from no sugar to ultrasweet. Suppose that only two firms have the necessary technology to manufacture breakfast cereals. What will they decide? To position themselves one beside the other, both making a medium-sweet product? Or move as far apart as possible, one selling a sugar-free cereal, the other a maxed out variety? The answer is far from trivial, for, as we saw with two ice-cream sellers (Chapter 9), two opposing forces are at work here. Moving closer to their rival enables them to serve more customers, but boosts competition and consequently reduces unit profit. Alternatively, moving further apart reduces potential demand, but also competition. One of the classic solutions to this problem is to differentiate a little, but not too much[5]: one manufacturer will market a moderately sweet cereal, the other a substantially sweeter one. Both parties are positioned halfway between the centre point on the segment and one of its ends.

The example above goes back to the very early days of breakfast cereals, when the challenge was to occupy undeveloped space. It has filled up since. Could it be too full? Many economists certainly think so.[6] This case was put to the Federal Trade Commission in a complaint lodged against the four big US manufacturers. The general idea is that in differentiated industries incumbents respond to the threat of new entrants by increasing the number of brands rather than cutting prices. For example, if they agree – as alleged in the complaint against the cereal firms – they can position themselves in such a way that demand is insufficient for a new entry to be profitable between themselves – or more exactly between their varieties – a sufficiently large distance to secure positive profits, but sufficiently small to ensure that a new entrant fitting itself between two varieties would lose money. According to the economists who worked alongside the FTC, a 'pre-emption' strategy of this sort is prejudicial to consumer interests.[7] It increases variety, which is not bad per se, because consumers like diversity. The worry is that the cost, and hence the price, of such surplus variety is too high, with manufacturers applying excessively high margins and lost scale economies.

Fast-Food Proliferation

But maybe you eat your breakfast at McDonald's and consequently have a more limited choice of cereals. In the present instance, we are going to look at the proliferation of fast-food outlets. In Canada's main cities, their number increased almost fourfold between the 1970s and early 2000s. Two economists have shown that without pre-emption strategies the increase would have been much smaller.[8] The likelihood of a new outlet – let's say a McDonald's – would drop depending on both the number of other McDonald's eateries in the vicinity and the number of existing competitors. In the first case, it would make sense to avoid cannibalization, a share of sales by the new outlet being lost by other eateries belonging to the same chain. In the second case, it would depend on the number of Burger Kings, Wendy's and such, because previously unsatisfied local demand is inevitably lower. But observation shows that new McDonald's do not follow this pattern. For example, all other things being equal, particularly demographics, opening a new McDonald's in an area where another McDonald's and one of its competitors are already operating is less frequent than when there is already another McDonald's and two of its competitors. The authors estimated that the average number of McDonald's observed in a given catchment area was twice as high as the theoretical model for opening outlets, without pre-emptive effects.

If the proliferation of breakfast cereals and McDonald's bemuses or irritates you, perhaps it's time to lift off for a real journey into space. The dietary options available to astronauts are much more limited.

Notes

1. Bruce, S. and Crawford, B. (1995), *Cerealizing America: The Unsweetened Story of American Breakfast Cereal*, Boston, MA: Faber and Faber.
2. Schultz, E. (2012), 'Cereal marketers race for global bowl domination', *Advertisting Age*.
3. Schmalensee, R. (1978), 'Entry deterrence in the ready-to-eat breakfast cereal industry', *Bell Journal of Economics*, 9: 305–327.
4. Lancaster, K. (1990), 'The economics of product variety: a survey', *Marketing Science*, 9: 189–206.
5. Gabszewicz, J. (2006), *La Différenciation des Produits*, Paris: Editions La Découverte.
6. Eaton, C. and Lipsey, R. (1979), 'The theory of market pre-emption: the persistence of excess capacity and monopoly in growing spatial markets', *Economica*, 46: 149–158.
7. Schmalensee, 'Entry deterrence in the ready-to-eat breakfast cereal industry', ibid.
8. Igami, M. and Yang, N. (2013), 'Cannibalization and pre-emptive entry of multi-product firms', *Rand Journal of Economics*, 36: 908–929.

ELEVEN

Four Wine-Economics Tasting Sessions

As a product, wine is unlike any other. At the very least, it tastes neither of coca nor vinegar. It is quite unusual in economic terms too, to such an extent that there is an economics journal in the United States devoted exclusively to the topic. Wine is no ordinary product for consumers, because they must make a purchase to gauge its quality and because, having drunk the wine, many of them will appreciate it only because they were told it was good. Furthermore, great wines are luxury goods, just like jewellery or handbags. These particular features give rise to competition that does not operate in quite the same way as in other markets. So I invite you to join me in tasting a few bottles of wine economics.

Session 1. The Ordinary Economy of Plonk

To underline the economic originality of quality wine it makes sense to start our round of tasting sessions with a glass or two of 'plonk'.

Wine retailed at €3 a bottle (in France) resembles many other ordinary supermarket products. Differentiation is slight, bearing on colour, grape variety, country of origin and brand name, such as Vieux Papes, a French red made with a blend of Merlot and Syrah grapes. These wines are standardized, with a constant taste and no surprises. They are produced and marketed on a large scale. The overall trend is for consumption of such wines to decline in longstanding wine-producing countries such as France, Italy or

Spain. In contrast, demand is growing in countries where wine consumption was less widespread.

New Zealand wines have proved particularly successful in the entry-level category.[1] Australia, New Zealand, Chile and California have capitalized on and developed a comparative advantage. With large areas of land available for planting vines and climatic conditions favouring high yields, these regions have turned wine growing and making into an industry. They are now the world's leading global exporters of wine. In 1817, to illustrate his theory of comparative advantage, David Ricardo showed that it was in England's interest to specialize in producing cloth, whereas Portugal would gain by focusing on wine. Today he would choose Australia, which sells much of its wine to the United Kingdom. On the other hand Algeria, in particular, has lost its former advantage. In the mid-twentieth century, it was the world's leading wine exporter, whereas it now barely features on the map.[2]

Taking a slightly closer, less macroscopic view, a small number of firms dominate the market for everyday wine. This is not immediately apparent because they hold an impressive brand portfolio. Just three companies dominate half the market in the United States, the world's biggest consumer of wine and the fourth largest producer.[3] Competition focuses on costs, reflected in a drive to identify and exploit economies of scale all the way along the value chain (vineyard management, wholesale purchasing of grapes and bulk wine, logistics, etc.), but with little differentiation (see above) and a modicum of product innovation (Tetra-Pak packaging, maturing with oak chips, peach or grapefruit-flavoured wines, etc.). Typically these companies have tended to move up-market. Constellation, for instance, has taken over Mondavi, one of California's leading wine growing and making ventures, known in particular for Opus One, a Napa Valley wine that fetches well over $100 a bottle. California is subject to keen competition from entry-level wines imported from Australia and Chile, but half the wine it now produces sells for over $10 a bottle.

To conclude our first tasting session, we should redress an injustice. The adoption by large wine producers of industrial methods has reduced costs, but it has also improved quality. It would be quite wrong to dismiss many of today's entry-level wines as 'plonk'.

Session 2. Is the Price of Wine an Indication of Its Quality?

Wine is what economists call an experience good, a concept referring to products the quality of which can only be determined by the consumer after purchase. In a much-cited article, George Akerlof, the winner of the Nobel prize for economics in 2001, showed that a competitive market is inefficient if buyers know less about the characteristics of goods than vendors. Good products are pushed aside to make room for bad ones. He used the example of second-hand cars.[4] The consumer has no idea whether they are dealing with an honest broker or a crook, whether the vehicle is a good deal or a lemon. So they are reluctant to pay the proper price for a car in good condition. Unable to sell their goods for what they are worth, the owners of decent vehicles desert the marketplace.

Resorting to expert advice is one way of limiting the extent of the problem. To avoid paying a high price for gut-rot plonk and make sure you find wine that is up to the mark, you may put your trust in wine buffs, guidebooks or your local vintner. There are plenty to choose from.

But can you rely on the experts who award points to wines and rank them after blind tastings? Yes, on the whole, providing you bear in mind that wine is an infinitely complex product. It contains dozens of acids, esters, aldehydes and sugars, not to mention minerals and other oligo-elements. Tasting wine is by no means an exact science. Experts may be inconsistent in their judgement, awarding different scores to the same bottle or falling into traps (like students at the Bordeaux wine faculty who identified notes of red berries in coloured white wines[5]). Are the experts credible? Here again, yes. For example, research has shown that Wine Spectator, the world's most popular wine magazine, does not award higher scores to wines advertised in its pages.[6]

Statistical analysis reveals that the scores awarded by experts rise according to the price of the wine, which they do not know. Connoisseurs add seven points (on a scale of 0 to 100) more to a wine that is 10 times more expensive than another one.[7] As this relationship is based on statistics, it is easy to find examples that contradict it. One of the best known instances is the 1976 Paris wine tasting, also known as the Judgement of Paris, though it has no connection with Helen of Troy. To mark the bicentennial of the American declaration of independence, eleven connoisseurs gathered in the French capital for a blind tasting of wines from California, Burgundy and Bordeaux.[8] Much to their surprise the first group did very well in the contest, the best marks for a white and a red going to California wines. Of the top four bottles of Chardonnay, three came from the USA. Yet prices varied by as much as one to five. On the other hand, non-specialists taking part in blind tastings are insensitive to price. In fact, they seem to award a higher score to cheaper wines.[9]

Session 3. Why Does the Price of Wine Influence Our Satisfaction?

In real life, as we say nowadays, we don't taste wine blind, and price exerts a surprising a priori influence. Presented, without being told, with two strictly identical wines but with different price tags in full view, consumers prefer the more expensive one. This preference is apparent in the judgement they report to the person supervising the experiment and by brain scans obtained from magnetic-resonance-imaging.[10] So you should have no qualms about telling your guests that the wine you're serving is expensive. They will enjoy it more!

There are two explanations for the correlation between price and satisfaction.

First, wine – or in the present case, fine wine – is a luxury good. It gives social distinction to the person purchasing and consuming it. This snobbism gives rise to very particular economic properties. Unlike everyday goods, demand increases as the price rises – the good becoming more desirable – and it increases more than proportionately to income – which is why billionaires are prepared to spend huge amounts of money to lay their hands on rare bottles of Romanée-Conti or Château Latour. Fine wine is in the same league as fast cars, jewellery and luxury handbags. It belongs to what are known as Veblen goods, a concept hatched to describe their two microeconomic oddities. We owe this notion to the eponymous US economist who published *The Theory of the Leisure Class* in 1899.

Secondly consumers tend to associate higher prices with higher quality. It is a handy pragmatic rule for assessing the characteristics of experience goods. In other words, price signals quality. The intuition behind this is that a higher priced good costs more to produce and is consequently of better quality. But consumers familiar with economic theory will also know that some vendors will deliberately increase their prices in order to pass a lemon off as something far superior. However the vendor too has a grasp of economic theory and knows they must lend credence to their price signal. Explaining that each bunch of grapes is only picked once it is ripe, that a horse is used rather than a tractor, or even that a helicopter has flown past to dry the vines before harvesting (a strange but existing practice) all help to make a price signal more credible.[11] Cost-cutting winegrowers who cheat can't compete with quality vineyards in this way.

Rounding off this session and the previous one, it is worth bearing in mind that consumers may benefit from the advice of experts, even if they don't share their preferences. The specialists can identify more expensive wines at blind tastings and consumers also prefer them, when they can see what they're drinking. Bear in mind too that the price of experience goods is not only an indication of the degree of competition; it also provides information on the quality of the product.

Session 4. Competition by Terroir and by Fraud

Let's end this wine-economics tasting session with two controversial topics.

Price is not the only quality signal picked up by consumers looking for a good bottle of wine. The label often indicates a specific geographical origin, maybe an appellation d'origine contrôlée or a prestigious clos or château. Two well-known examples of terroir certification are the 1855 classification of Bordeaux grand crus and Burgundy climats.

Information on the geographical origin of a wine may or may not help consumers. On the one hand, it reduces the risk, pinpointed by Akerlof, of bad products driving out good ones. On the other, it limits competition. It raises a barrier to (market) entry because winegrowers whose land is outside the appellation cannot use the name. Philippe de Rothschild, the owner of Château Mouton, campaigned for years to have his wine upgraded from second to first growth Bordeaux.

As far as most winegrowers in the New World are concerned, the terroir concept is an excuse for protectionism, barring the way to recognition of their best wines and efforts to improve quality. In short, down with rentiers and those who claim that the quality of a great wine is rooted in the characteristics of the soil and microclimate of specific vineyards, rather than grape variety and vinification techniques. The Judgement of Paris and other blind tastings of wines from California and the Old World that have followed suit tend to endorse this view.[12] On the other hand, the econometric studies of the link between wine quality and terroir have been inconclusive. For example, an article on Haut Médoc wine shows that the quality does not depend on terroir but on winegrowing techniques,[13] whereas another, devoted to the Mosel valley observed that the physical conditions of properties (exposure to sun, slope, elevation) are key determinants of wine quality.[14] It is still an open question. In a way, it doesn't matter because a prestigious geographical origin has a similar effect to a high price, enhancing consumer satisfaction.

As a luxury experience, good fine wine is a target for fraud. Only two barrels of Romanée-Conti were produced in 1945. Yet over the last 25 years the equivalent of about 10 barrels have been sold! According to one estimate, 5% of the wine sold at auctions is fake.[15] The potential gains are high and forgery is relatively easy, yet hard to detect, so there is a big temptation to produce fake grand crus. Stick a label marked Château Lafite 1982, an exceptional vintage, on a bottle of Château Lafite 1975, a poor year, or fill an empty bottle borrowed from a first growth wine with rather more humdrum beverage, reseal it and away you go. There is little likelihood of being caught. Many collectors don't actually drink the wine they buy, and if they do the quality of vintage wines varies a great deal from one bottle to the next, so it's hard to say if the wine is really what it claims to be. Oddly enough, the most difficult vintages to find on the market were made in mediocre years. As a general rule, wine from poor years is consumed sooner than wine from the best years, so several decades later it becomes a rarity. At the same time these vintages are much sought after by enthusiasts trying to build a 'vertical' collection, with every vintage of a single grand cru. In this particular case, a high price signals poorer quality!

In 2016, the American Association of Wine Economists held its annual conference in Bordeaux.[16] Two days of academic debate were crowned by a firework display on Place de la Bourse. The next day participants visited various grand cru wineries. Specializing in the economics of wine, rather than public transit for instance, does bring a few perks!

Notes

1. Schirmer, R. (2012), 'Un nouveau monde des vins, enquêtes et témoignages', Groupe de Recherche pour l'Education et la Prospective, 115–121.
2. Meloni, G. and Swinnen, J. (2014), 'The rise and fall of the world's largest wine exporter – and its institutional legacy', *Journal of Wine Economics*, 9: 3–33.
3. McMillan, R. (2016), *State of the Wine Industry*, Silicon Valley Bank wine division.
4. Akerlof, G. (1970), 'The market for "lemons": quality uncertainty and the market mechanism', *Quarterly Journal of Economics*, 84: 488–500.
5. Brochet, F., Dubourdieu, D. and Morrot, G. (2001), 'The color of odors', *Brain and Language*, 79: 309–320.
6. Reuter, J. (2009), 'Does advertising bias product reviews? An analysis of wine ratings', *Journal of Wine Economics*, 4: 125–151.
7. Goldstein, R. et al. (2008), 'Do more expensive wines taste better? Evidence from a large sample of blind tastings', American Association of Wine Economists, working paper 16.
8. https://en.wikipedia.org/wiki/Judgment_of_Paris_(wine)
9. Goldstein et al., 'Do more expensive wines taste better?, ibid.
10. Plassmann H. et al. (2008), 'Marketing actions can modulate neural representations of experienced pleasantness', *Proceedings of the National Academy of Sciences*, 105: 1050–1054.
11. Mahenc, P. and Meunier, V. (2006), 'Early sales of Bordeaux grands crus', *Journal of Wine Economics*, 1: 57–74.
12. www.wine-economics.org/the-judgment-of-princeton.
13. Gergaud, O. and Ginsburgh, V. (2012), 'Natural endowments, production technologies and the quality of wines in Bordeaux. Does terroir matter?', *Journal of Wine Economics*, 5: 3–21.
14. Ashenfelter, O. and Storchmann, K. (2010), 'Measuring the economic effect of global warming on viticulture using auction, retail and wholesale prices', American Association of Wine Economists, working paper 60.
15. 'Château Lafake. The fine-wine boom is attracting forgers', *The Economist*, 16 June 2011.
16. www.wine-economics.org.

TWELVE

Intermezzo

No End of Differentiation

We are now living in a world of massive differentiation. But what difference does that make to competition? All the difference in the world, from a theoretical point of view, because differentiation leads to imperfect competition. Let's look at this in greater detail.

Competition Through Differentiation

Monopolistic competition, a term hatched by the American economist Edward Chamberlin in the 1930s, sums up the economics of differentiation. On the one hand, companies manufacturing variants of the same product are clearly in competition, yet on the other hand, they enjoy a monopoly. This apparent contradiction is easily explained: each seller, thanks to the particularities of their product, controls part of the market while remaining subject to competition from sellers of similar products. Just think of cola-flavoured sodas: Coca-Cola benefits from having a captive customer base, which will only give up its favourite beverage if Pepsi Cola sells for a much lower price. In other words, a can of Pepsi and a can of Coke are not completely substitutable. As we saw in Chapter 7 the differences are not so much a matter of taste – in a blind test most consumers can't tell the difference between the two – as of branding and the image it projects through advertising.

The connection between substitutability and competitive intensity is very intuitive. When two companies market very similar variants of the same product, only a very slight difference in price is sufficient for all the consumers to buy the cheaper variant; so competition is intense. On the other hand, if the variants are substantially different a company that lowers its price will not succeed in luring all the consumers away from the competition. So competition is moderate here. Each company enjoys a sort of local monopoly. In a general way, the more variants are differentiated, the less intensive competition will be. This statement links up with the one in Chapter 6 stating that competitive intensity decreases with the number of companies in the market. Differentiation is at least as powerful a factor for competition as the number of sellers. In my view it is actually more powerful, because it is more robust. Competitive intensity may be at its peak when only two companies dominate the market, but it will never be as intense if their respective products are differentiated. So when studying the competition, make sure you check the extent of product differentiation before identifying the number of market players.

Competition through differentiation is a particular form of imperfect competition. Companies are no longer passive players; they frame and deploy strategies, particularly on pricing, and their strategies make allowance for what the others are doing. This gives them market power, in other words the capacity to sell at above marginal cost. A company differentiates its product in order to enjoy the greatest possible local monopoly. But its competitors respond by trying to produce similar variants in order to capture the largest possible share of the market. The company is subject to two forms of pressure: one forces it to differentiate its product as far as possible to maximize margin per unit; the other forces it to market variants similar to its competitors' in order to cater for the largest share of the market and thus maximize the volume of sales.

The term 'monopolistic competition' is clearly particularly apt, and better than the notion of imperfect competition proposed by economists in reference to the perfect-competition model. Imperfect competition suggests that consumers inevitably lose out and that everyone would fare much better if perfect competition prevailed. In a world without differentiation there would be only one car model, only one type of mobile phone and even only one sort of cruise. I'm not sure consumers would be too thrilled. To rephrase Chamberlin, faced with demand for diversity perfect competition turns out not to be ideal, indeed it is a departure from it.[1]

But why do we feel the need for several variants of the same product? Because, as consumers, we are not all the same. Our tastes and consequently consumer preferences diverge, as does our income. Let's do a simple exercise.[2] Just imagine, on the contrary, a world in which all consumers were identical in terms of both preferences and means. There would be no reason to manufacture cars of various colours; all the houses would be much the same. Nor would there be luxury variants and standard products.

Going to the opposite extreme, why isn't there a variant for each consumer? Simply because of the cost of production. In general, it costs much less to manufacture several completely identical items than a unique one. It often takes very long production runs to achieve the lowest cost per unit, manufacturing for instance tens or even hundreds of thousands of identical items a year in the same factory. Thanks to the economies of scale yielded by repeated production of the same good, a company can offer a lower price, which, in the eyes of the consumer, will more than make up for their displeasure at not acquiring a variant perfectly suited to their wishes. The tension between economies of scale and variety explains, for instance, why there are only a few thousand breakfast-cereal variants, rather than several billion. In Chapter 10, which is devoted to them, we saw how differentiation between products is comparable to spatial differentiation.

Multi-Product and Multi-Variant Oligopolies

In all the industries we have studied in the preceding chapters (cruises, toys, wine, cereals, sodas), consumers can choose from a wide variety of products. There is considerable differentiation. Moreover, these industries are generally dominated by a small number of firms which have diversified to market several products, own several brands and offer a whole range of variants. Take PepsiCo for instance. You are familiar with this firm because of its flagship brand of soda and variants such as Diet Pepsi, Pepsi Max and Pepsi Next. But you probably didn't know that it also has interests in orange juice, lemonade, bottled mineral water, breakfast cereals and even crisps, through various brands such as Tropicana, 7up, Aquafina and Doritos, with many variants. Nor did you know that Coca Cola sells more than 200 products in Japan, many of which you won't find elsewhere.[3]

This type of concentrated industry dominates international trade and the United States, though maybe not the whole world. With few companies in this league and high differentiation, they can generate high margins.

Exchanges of the same product between different countries account for a substantial part of international trade. For example, new cars are shipped in both directions between the USA and Germany, or between Germany and France. For a long time, economic theory was unable to explain this intrasectoral trade; on the contrary it predicted that each country would specialize in producing such and such a product, depending on its comparative advantages. The monopolistic-competition model that has been incorporated into the theory of international trade has enabled us to understand this situation. We owe the original ideal to Paul Krugman, winner of the Nobel prize for economics in 2008 and a well-known *New York Times* columnist. Companies in one country sell differentiated goods and specialize in the production of certain variants: large saloons in

Germany, for instance; pick-ups in the USA; smaller models in France.

Whether it is intersectoral or not, international trade is fed by a very small number of companies with very specific characteristics. We now have a pretty clear picture of their identity, thanks to US statistics and research.[4] Just four in every thousand (0.4%) businesses in the USA account for 96% of all exports. They are larger and more productive, pay higher wages, and have greater assets than companies catering only for the home market. They share these features with the big importers too, for the simple reason that they generally export and import. Of all US exporters, the top centile alone accounts for 80% of all exports. Firms exporting goods to five or more countries generate 92% of US exports by value. To complete this account, we should point out that a quarter of all US exporters export more than five different products, generating 98% of the value of exports.

It is highly likely that these characteristics may be extrapolated to the companies in other countries that play an active part in international trade. The available data is less complete but confirms the overall trend.[5] What we once called multinational, then transnational and now more generally global firms are giant, multi-product undertakings. Of course there are exceptions to this rule. Lego, for instance, the world's second largest toy manufacturer (see Chapter 9), only sells one type of product. It manufactures bricks and boxes of bricks; nothing else. It did at one point venture into theme parks, but soon dropped the idea when it failed to take off.

No work has so far been published assessing the degree of product differentiation in these companies. But there are three good reasons for assuming it is high.

First, raw materials now longer dominate international trade, most of them counting as commodities. They are consequently the opposite of a differentiated good, as you will recall (see Chapter 1). Many consumer goods have taken their place. Think of toys, for example, four-fifths of which are made in China. And, as we have seen, final consumer goods are differentiated. This includes goods that may be confused with their brand-name. Pringles crackers have been identified as the only mass-consumption product that is completely standardized from one end of the globe to the other.[6] Even Coca-Cola is not quite the same from one country to the next.

Second, new consumers, mainly in emerging economies, are joining the existing mass, and much as everyone else they have different tastes and preferences. Just one example is sufficient to illustrate this point: the cruise industry is taking off in China, but Chinese tourists want shorter holidays than their US or European counterparts.

Last but not least, distance is not dead, as we saw in the intermezzo concluding Part I. Yet, at the risk of repeating ourselves, spatial differentiation is merely another form of differentiation.

There is a clear link between large firms and highly concentrated market sectors. Concentration is conventionally gauged by the combined market share of the top four companies, or C4, in a given market. Here again we should look particularly at the USA because this indicator has been monitored since 1997 for key industrial sectors. There are nearly a thousand in all, ranging from wholesaling of recyclable materials to cocoa-bean processing and chocolate manufacture, through casinos. In 2012, the C4 of industry as a whole was about one-third. That may seem quite low, but bear in mind that the sectoral breakdown is approximate in terms of competition. An industry may encompass companies that are not rivals because they are operating in separate markets. Among the most highly concentrated sectors (C4 of over 80%) we find, predictably, mass retailing, aerospace and tobacco manufacturing. But we also find firms producing dairy butter, office supplies, handbags or ammunition for rifles and handguns. We should also stress that the concentration measured here is increasing, rising by 15% in 10 years.[7]

However, statistical offices have not published any indicators monitoring the increasing role of differentiation in consumer goods. So it is not systematically documented, though we all have some experience of its effects. If you are into skiing, just think of the range of different skis on offer. If you have children, consider the number of soft toys or board games that might appeal to your kids, while recalling how it 'used' to be, say in the 1980s. Surely choice was more limited then? In any case, as we may suspect, differentiation exerts increasing power and there is no sign of it stopping soon. The harvest of consumer data, thanks in particular to online purchases, is increasingly diverse and accurate. Companies are gaining a clearer idea of individual preferences. Those 'people who liked this, also liked' messages are not just designed to sell other goods to the same consumer. The same data can be used to develop new variants they will 'like'.

The lack of data no doubt explains why emphasis is placed on the size of companies and on concentration, without taking into account the variety of products sold by oligopolistic giants. Economists are also partly responsible for the lack of connection between concentration and differentiation. The basic models described in textbooks study these two trends separately. They posit, for example, that each company only manufactures a single variant of the differentiated product, whereas in practice there is nothing stopping a company from offering several variants to cater for consumer preferences, regardless of the fact that variants may cannibalize one another, at least in part. This is the case when a Starbucks or McDonald's opens near another store belonging to the same chain, or with the many breakfast-cereal brands marketed by Kellogg's or General Mills. Saturating urban space or product features may be an effective corporate strategy for preventing competitors from entering the market (see Chapter 10).

Contrary to what is often asserted, mass consumption is not synonymous with standardization. Differentiation of final-consumption products has become massive. In combination with high concentration this may undermine competition. But the predominance of multi-product, multi-variant oligopolies may benefit consumers too. Such firms cut costs, through economies of scale, range and learning, which they pass on to consumers, while at the same time fulfilling their demands for variety.

Notes

1. 'Thus, wherever there is a demand for diversity of product, pure competition turns out not to be the ideal, but a departure from it.' Lecture by Edward Chamberlin in 1949 at the American Economic Association; Chamberlin, E. (1950), 'Product Heterogeneity and Public Policy', *The American Economic Review*, 40(2): 92.
2. Gabszewicz J. (2006), *La Différenciation des Produits*, Paris: Editions La Découverte.
3. Ghemawat, P. (2010), 'The globalization of markets', in Globalization notes series, IESE insights.
4. Bernard, A., Jensen, B., Redding, S. and Schott, P. (2007), 'Firms in international trade', *Journal of Economic Perspectives*, 21: 105–130.
5. Statistical insights: Who's Who in International Trade. A Spotlight on OECD Trade by Enterprise Characteristics Data (2016), OECD Insights.
6. Ghemawat, 'The globalization of markets', ibid.
7. 'Too much of a good thing, profits are too high. America needs a giant dose of competition', *The Economist*, 26 March 2016.

PART III

Competition and Innovation

[...] the competition from the new commodity, the new technology, the new source of supply, the new type of organization [...] the competition which commands a decisive cost or quality advantage and which strikes not at the margins of the profits and the outputs of the existing firms but at their foundations and their very lives. This kind of competition is as much more effective than the other as a bombardment is in comparison with forcing a door, and so much more important that it becomes a matter of comparative indifference whether competition in the ordinary sense functions more or less promptly; the powerful lever that in the long run expands output and brings down prices is in any case made of other stuff.

Joseph Schumpeter, *Capitalism, Socialism and Democracy*, 1942

With innovation, competition shifts into a new dimension. It becomes dynamic, moving away from the stable world of ordinary rivalry and into a more tumultuous, uncertain place. One might reasonably expect this dynamic world to operate over the long term, but with the accelerating pace of innovation today there seems good cause to doubt this.

As innovation gathers momentum, we soon see its effects on competition: an increasingly large number of consumers rush to adopt new products and services, shunning older goods; in the meantime some established companies are overwhelmed and gradually sidelined by the new entrants. We shall see numerous examples of this trend in the following chapters. Creating and destroying wealth in one fell swoop this process is known as disruption or uberization.

THIRTEEN

Uberizing the Razor

Is it possible to dent the supremacy of Gillette in the razor market? Yes, by applying a simple idea: send spare blades by post every month to consumers' homes. People signing up for this service no longer need to go to a supermarket and can shave at half the price. Taking its cue from Amazon, for delivery, and Netflix, for its reasonably priced monthly subscription, this business model has already conquered 7% of the American market for razors.

Meet Michael Dubin, the Jeff Bezos of shaving. He launched Dollar Shave Club in 2012, scoring immediate success with a hilarious video. A few years latter his company boasted 3 million subscribers paying a monthly fee of a few dollars. Gillette, the world leader for razors, has responded by starting its own online store and suing Dollar Shave Club, alleging that the startup has infringed one of its many patents. In 2016, Michael Dubin sold his company to Unilever for $1 billion.

The Economics of Razors, a Textbook Example

Razors and their blades, or more recently cartridges, are a bit of a fetish for economic theory, giving rise to models published in leading academic journals. They rate a mention in every course on advanced microeconomics. The reason is simple. Apart from the fact that most economists are men (so far out of the 79 people to be awarded the Nobel prize for economics, only one is a woman), razors are an ideal basis for studying various economic phenomena. First, competition between system goods: a razor (handle) with no blade is no use at all, and vice-versa. Second, the problems posed by incompatibility: Gillette's Mach 3 cartridges won't fit on a Schick Hydro 3 handle. Third the benefits of standardization: previous-generation 'safety' razors work with double-edge blades manufactured by various firms. Lastly the competitive advantages of an installed base: the more people own a Wilkinson Sword Quattro Titanium handle, the more they will buy the corresponding blades.

The economic renown of the razor is such that the business model based on subsidizing a good in order to make a profit on another one is sometimes referred to as razor and blade. It might more specifically have been named after Gillette, even though, contrary to popular belief, it did not choose to play this particular hand at the beginning of the twentieth century.[1] However for many years it did mail a razor to young men in the USA on their eighteenth birthday, in order to generate revenue on subsequent, recurrent sales of blades.

Building a System on Incompatibility

To successfully deploy a strategy of this sort, a company must block any form of compatibility with products other than its own. The company would be doomed if its competitors could market blades of the same quality fitting the handle it gave away for free: either it includes the cost of the handle in the price it sets for its blades, which would mean not selling any of them; or it sells its blades at the same price as the competition, leaving it no way of recouping the money lost on the handle. Incompatibility may be technical. Countless consumers must have come home from the supermarket with blades that don't fit on their razor or their partner's. Incompatibility may also be legal in origin, a company holding patents that protect it from market entry by competitors wishing to imitate its product.

But incompatible products do not exclude competition; it merely operates between closed systems: Nespresso coffee machines and capsules versus the Senseo equivalent; Epson or Canon printers and ink cartridges; Microsoft, Sony or Nintendo video-game consoles, and so on. From a static point of view, competition focuses on recruiting consumers, which explains the sky-high marketing and advertising budgets to lure them on board. So it should no longer come as a surprise to see David Beckham in a TV advert for Gillette, to learn that shaving is an emotionally charged experience, or indeed to be dazzled by the garish colours of the packaging on your first handle and blades.

In the longer term, competition hinges on innovation: razor cartridges with twin stainless steel blades, with three blades and a lubricating strip, with a plastic comfort guard, and such. These days you can even find a razor with six blades and another fitted with a handle containing a battery that produces soothing micro-pulsations to 'improve razor glide', and ball technology that 'pivots over the contours of your face'. It is hardly surprising that a technology race of this intensity, centring on a pretty humdrum product, has prompted mockery and consternation.[2]

Incumbent Innovation and Its Limits

We should start by pointing out that there are good reasons for prioritizing technology. It is no easy matter cutting 10,000 to 15,000 hard-as-steel strands of facial hair, growing in all directions on an uneven surface. Then there is the issue of cost and price. Each new model is launched with spare cartridges, each costing more than their predecessors. Manufacturing costs go up as the product becomes more technically sophisticated, but they also fall thanks to economies of learning and streamlined processes.

In the absence of published data, it is hard to determine which of these trends prevails. Either way, manufacturing costs only account for a small share of the sales price of blade cartridges. According to a *Daily Mail* survey in 2009, production costs represent only 2% of the retail price of a packet of four Fusion Power cartridges. Packaging costs 1% of the total, with 13% for value-added tax, 19% for the retailer's gross margin and the rest for Gillette.

The continuous innovation we see in wet-shave razors corresponds to a well-known dynamic which was modelled by Clayton M Christensen, a Professor of Business Administration at the Harvard Business School. In a best-selling book he contrasted the 'incumbent' innovation of established corporations to the 'disruptive' innovation of upstart new entrants.[3] Established firms are concerned with constantly improving the performance of their products to lure buyers away from the competition and encourage their own customers to adopt more expensive models. Products and customers gradually move up-market. This sort of innovation is based on economies of scale, research and development, and a good grasp of which customers generate the most profits, or are likely to do so.

Disruptive Innovation Bares Its Teeth

As a result, established companies pay too little attention to down-market demand, to technology breakthroughs and business models from other sectors. It is often too late when they finally see them coming. A key characteristic of companies acting on disruptive innovations is that they start by taking an interest in sidelined consumers, offering them a cheaper product that delivers only mediocre performance but does have a 'new' feature, with additional appeal. They then move up-market by improving conventional performance and start poaching on the preserve of established firms, so much so that they sometimes become a threat to the latters' survival.

Dollar Shave Club took precisely this course. It started by targeting young, down-at-heel consumers who were fed up with the price of cartridges in shops and the hassle of getting hold of them. Initially, Dollar Shave Club only marketed twin-blade razors, with a dollar-a-month plan covering five cartridges and a free handle. It went on to diversify the range, offering models with four or six blades, at a price of $6 to $9 a month. Its base costs are low because, much as for the in-house razors sold by big retailers such as Walmart or Carrefour, it is supplied by little known sources such as the South Korean razor-and-blades manufacturer Dorco.

The new feature is home delivery, which has several advantages for many customers. No longer any need to remember to buy replacement cartridges, at the risk of running out just when you need to be clean-shaven. No need to go to the shops, sometimes just for blades. No more security hassles, with the obligation to find a sales assistant to open the razor-and-blades display cabinet or to get the person at the till to remove the plastic box guarding the goods against theft. No longer any fear of being suspected of having stolen what you have actually purchased, nor of having acquired some hazardous, illegal merchandise. Dollar Shave Club has highlighted all these advantages in crazy viral videos.

Gillette, which holds a 70% share of the US razor market, was slow to respond, probably for the general reasons cited by Christensen. Most of the time established firms lack agility, trusting blindly in incumbent innovation and customers who show a good return. Only three years later did the firm roll out the Gillette Shave Club, copying Dubin's business model.

Gillette Counter-Attacks

Gillette filed a lawsuit against Dollar Shave Club at the US District Court of Delaware in December 2015. It alleged that the start-up was infringing a patent registered in 2004 covering the special coating that reduces blade-wear. It asked the court to suspend sales by its competitor. As is always, the case legal action of this sort can be interpreted in two ways: either Gillette is defending its legitimate position or it is trying to bankrupt a firm that is emerging as a serious rival.

In the first case, Gillette's patent is watertight and Dollar Shave Club has really infringed it, jeopardizing the return on investment in R&D that the former is entitled to expect. In the second case, the patent does not stand up or has not been infringed by the start-up (which Gillette may well know). But it may be hoping to undermine its competitor's position. Though still a small company, it would inevitably have to shoulder massive legal costs with considerable judicial uncertainty weighing on its operations for years. If so, this ploy has not paid off, the Anglo-Dutch consumer-goods company Unilever having taken over Dollar Shave Club.

We have no firm basis for preferring one or other interpretation. Until such time as the court issues a ruling, or Gillette and Unilever reach an out-of-court settlement, European readers tempted by the Dollar Shave Club service will have to bide their time as, unlike Uber, it is only available in the USA. But don't get in a lather, for in France Big Moustache has been supplying subscribers since 2013 and, believe it or not, in the United Kingdom there is a Sterling Shave Club.

Notes

1. Picker, R. (2010), 'The Razors-and-blades myth(s)', University of Chicago Law & Economics, Olin working paper 532.
2. Roose, K. (2014), 'Gillette s new razor XE "razor" is everything that's wrong with American innovation', *New York Magazine*.
3. Christensen, C. (1997), *The Innovator's Dilemma: When New Technologies Cause Great Firms to Fail*, Boston, MA: Harvard Business School Press.

FOURTEEN

Coaches, BlaBlaCar and Trains

For many years, the only long-distance solution for people without a car in some countries was to hitch or catch a train. Then came car-pooling. With Internet access they could link up with others to travel cheaply. Now there are coaches, painted in garish colours, dashing all over the country. And in the transport industry, contrary to the moral of the fable, one must be as swift as a hare and make a timely start!

On the Starting Line

Cross-country coach services started in France after BlaBlaCar, the ride-sharing platform. They were part of the so-called Macron Act, a series of measures promoting growth, business and equal economic opportunity voted into law in August 2015 at the instigation of then-Finance Minister Emmanuel Macron. In so doing, France's future President liberalized long-distance coach transport. In the starting blocks were established operators and new entrants. The first group included Ouibus, formerly iDbus and a subsidiary of French Rail, and Eurolines, part of the Transdev group. These firms had been running international services for quite some time, for instance from Paris to Lisbon. Taking advantage of a legal loophole,[1] they could pick up passengers in France on their way through and consequently sell tickets for stops in-between, say Paris to Bordeaux. Among the new entrants were Flixbus, a German coach operator and Starshipper, a consortium of local French companies.

The race to open new routes got off to an explosive start.[2] The number of possible connections and towns served doubled over the first five months. Coaches carried 641,500 passengers in the last quarter of 2015, five times more than the previous quarter. Obviously, the new entrants had to run even faster than their competitors to develop their networks. Flixbus started with five services in France, opening another 239 in just a few months, whereas Eurolines and its national subsidiary started with 441 services, adding 94 more.

With six operators on the starting line, competition was intense, particularly as some were bound to be eliminated. In Germany, where the market was deregulated two years earlier, the situation already resembles a duopoly, perhaps even a monopoly, the two largest coach companies having merged, taking a 70% market share. The nearest competitor only has a 12% share. Another company, a subsidiary of a British firm, has thrown in the sponge. Yet another went bankrupt, but has been taken over, with just 2% market share. In the United Kingdom, twenty years after coach transport was liberalized, there are only two main operators. And in Sweden, fifteen years after the market was opened up, three companies dominate the business.

An Adaptable, Modular Market

Savings related to their size or network are not the main reason for the small number of operators in national markets, once they have reached cruising speed. Coach transport requires vehicles, drivers and ticket offices, but without the long-term fixed costs associated with an order for a large fleet of high-speed trains. The only potential source of economies of scale is the booking system, which is now electronic, but it is easier to recoup the initial investment in a software platform with a large number of customers. No substantial savings can be made on the network itself. An operator runs a service from A to B, without necessarily connecting to other parts of its network.

At an operational level, coach transport is adaptable and modular. Growth can be incremental – launching a new route, purchasing new vehicles to run on it, hiring drivers, then starting the same process for another route. Moreover, if a new route does not live up to expectations, the coaches can be allocated to another route, or sold second-hand. It offers far greater flexibility and lower risk than rail transport, and any risk is shared because firms such as Flixbus or Ouibus make ample use of subcontracting. Coaches may sport the national operator's colours and catchy brand name, but they often belong to small or medium-sized companies and are driven by their employees.

Branding is the main reason for the limited number of operators once a market stabilizes. Coach passengers are not regular, frequent customers. They only use this mode of transport a few times a year. Very few travel by coach on the same route every week. So a large part of the population must be familiar with the available operators. The latter must achieve widespread brand recognition and maintain it all over the country. We should note in passing that the more routes a company operates, the more coaches it will have publicizing its name and the more the general public will see it on the roads, thus boosting brand recognition among potential users, who in due course will think of it for a journey by coach. Size adds to size, and publicity is essential in the race to grow by extending the number of routes.

Entering the Race Is Very Expensive

Six operators on the starting line is a lot, if you think of the net cost of competing in the first stage of the race. In 2017, coach operators in France were running at a loss. The investments needed to enter and develop the market explain most of this shortfall. But in some cases, losses have been aggravated by very low ticket prices, which do not even cover operating costs. In 2016, average revenue per passenger was €12 for an average distance of 376 kilometres.[3] Which is not much! Furthermore, coaches are far from being full. Average occupancy is about one-third and at present only 5% of routes do better than 60%. Meanwhile, a journey costs the coach operator exactly the same, whether the vehicle is full or two-thirds empty.

In the drive to outdo the competition and win market share, prices have substantially dropped during the first stage of the race. There are many promotional offers, some really impressive, with plenty of scope for picking up €1 rides. The price of coach transport in France was almost halved between July 2015, the last month before liberalization, and February 2016. It seems plausible to assume that the price per passenger-kilometre fell more steeply on the routes with the most competitors. The relevant data is not yet available in France, but in Germany the price per passenger-kilometre observed on routes operated by a single company is higher than on routes served by two operators, itself higher than on routes with three operators. These findings were corroborated by detailed econometric research, which concluded that, all the other characteristics of the route being equal (such as length and number of stops), the average price per passenger-kilometre decreases by 5.6% for each additional operator.[4]

In 2015, half of all the routes in France were operated by just one company. At the other extreme, six companies serve the Paris-Angers route.[5] But it would be a mistake to conclude that competition is generally weak. The truth of the matter is that demand on most routes is too low to attract more than one operator. In addition, it is essential to make allowance for traffic. There are at least four operators serving the ten busiest routes, which account for half of overall demand. One last figure, if you can stand it: 86% of passengers travelled on a route subject to competition.

Severely Selective Competition

So why are there more contenders at the start of the race than at the finish? The immediate answer is that competition imposes a form of selection on companies. The ones that perform least well – in their choice of routes and the frequency of service, in hiring subcontractors, winning over customers with advertising, or indeed setting prices and controlling costs – are knocked out of the market. To this we must add a bias familiar to economists. Before deciding to enter a market, a company weighs up its chances of success and the corresponding profits, as well as its chances of failure and the corresponding losses. For example, with a one-in-two chance of winning 100 and the same odds for losing 90, it will decide to go ahead, in the expectation of winning 5 ([0.5x100] – [0.5x90]). On the other hand it makes no allowance for the effect of its entry on the other contenders, reducing their chances of success. All in all, it is as if each player was overly optimistic, which explains why there are more contenders.

BlaBlaCar launched several years before the coaches (if we overlook its previous existence as a slow-growth community website which started in 2004 as Covoiturage.fr). The firm now transports more than 10 million people a quarter in about twenty countries. The term 'transport' may be seem inappropriate in so far that all that BlaBlaCar actually does is connect, via the net, passengers and people driving their own vehicle. Strictly speaking it doesn't transport anybody, but the services it provides are essential for long-distance car-pooling to become a mode of mass transport: easy, reliable booking; user trust; convenient, guaranteed payment; and of course a huge range of trips on offer. Tomorrow on the Paris-Lyon route, for example, you may choose from 75 rides, the first leaving at 4.10, and the last one at 22.00.

The Hard Life of Long-Distance Car-Pooling

It doesn't take long to analyse the competitive race between car-pooling companies: it's a winner-takes-all game and BlaBlaCar won. In France, of course, but also in Europe and maybe in India or Mexico in the future. The winner-takes-all phenomenon is a well-known feature of the economics of Internet platforms,[6] intermediaries connecting up two sides of the market. In the present case, this means drivers and passengers, the former wishing to fill their car in order to share the expense of a particular journey, the latter wanting to make the trip cheaply. Obviously, the more drivers there are posting rides on a specific car-pooling site, the more likely it will be for passengers looking for a ride to find what they need there – which they would be well advised to browse – and the more riders browsing the site, the better the chances are that a driver will find passengers there, prompting them to post plans of their journey. In other words, the more customers, or buyers, there are on one side of the market, the more attractive the site will be for customers, or providers, on the other side of the market, this property gaining strength of its own accord. This snowball effect (see Chapter 15) benefits the trading platform that started first with good quality of service, or more exactly that started at the right time. Momentum is so crucial that the most effective image is that of an avalanche: it is hard to know beforehand when the market will start to move; indeed there is no absolute certainty it will ever occur! BlaBlaCar won because, after being a tortoise for a few years, it turned into a hare at just the right time. It didn't invent car-pooling, but it found out how to speed up its growth. It made this leap in 2012, when it adopted a business model based on taking a commission on every journey. In so doing, it increased its investment capacity tenfold.

With recurrent revenue a startup can raise venture-capital funds. At its most recent funding round, BlaBlaCar had no difficulty raising $200 million.

BlaBlaCar's development in France was also helped by the favourable competitive climate, rail travel being expensive and long-distance coaches virtually non-existent.

For many years SNCF (French Rail) has put the priority on speed and a booking system with dynamic pricing that makes late reservations more expensive. It has consequently disregarded some customers, primarily those with low incomes, but also those with no need to hurry or who only decide to travel at the last moment. The socio-economic characteristics of car-pool passengers are consequently fairly predictable: they are younger, less well off and more urban than the French average; the unemployed are over-represented, as are single people living alone.[7] Drivers have a similar profile, though more of them are in work and they are slightly older. By far the most frequently cited reason for opting to car-pool is that it costs less than travelling by train. One in two passengers stated that they would travel less if car-pooling was not available. When not available they would travel, in descending order of preference, on an ordinary train, a high-speed train or lastly by car. They did not mention coaches, because the survey was carried out before liberalization.

An additional factor contributing to BlaBlaCar's growth was the lack of coach transport. Much as car-pooling, this mode appeals to people left stranded by the railways. But with current prices, coach travel is 30% less expensive than even car-pooling, on average. Of course, it is slower too. On motorways in France, the speed limit for coaches is 100 kph and they make frequent stops. Furthermore, they often deliver their passengers to parts of town that are not easily accessible, there still being a shortage of proper coach stations. On the other hand, coaches are more comfortable, with more space for luggage. Some may prefer WiFi access to the almost inevitable chat with the driver and fellow passengers.

The future will show how competition will balance out between the two modes of transport, in terms of both service differentiation and price. We may nevertheless predict that the price of coach transport will rise and that of car-pooling fall. Concentration has occurred among coach operators and is likely to continue. There were six in the starting blocks, half that number three years later. In due course they will raise prices to cover all their costs, at least. On routes where competition from coaches is strong, car-pooling drivers may well trim their rates, it generally being preferable to share a little rather than not at all.

The first railways opened almost two centuries ago. Rail transport has since had to compete with cars and planes. Now it must come to terms with BlaBlaCar and coaches. Just as in the past, it will pull through, even if it loses many customers. But unlike the fabled tortoise, it won't win the race against these two hares.

Notes

1. Ruling 14-A-05, dated 27 February 2014, on competitive operation of the market for regular inter-regional coach services, Autorité de la Concurrence [French fair-trading regulator].
2. *Analyse du Marché Libéralisé des Services Interurbains par Autocar*, third and fourth quarters of 2015, Autorité de Régulation des Activités Ferroviaires et Routières [French road and rail transport regulator].
3. *Analyse du Marché Libéralisé des Services Interurbains par Autocar*, Autorité de Régulation des Activités Ferroviaires et Routières, ibid.
4. Dürrv N., Heim, S. and Hüschelrath, K. (2015), 'Deregulation, competition and consolidation: the case of the German interurban bus industry', discussion paper 15–061, Zentrum für Europäische Wirtschaftforschung.
5. *Analyse du Marché Libéralisé des Services Interurbains par Autocar*, Autorité de Régulation des Activités Ferroviaires et Routières, ibid.
6. Evans, D. (ed.) (2011), *Platform Economics: Essays on Multi-sided Businesses*, Competition Policy International.
7. Enquête auprès des Utilisateurs du Covoiturage Longue Distance (2015), Agence de l'Environnement et de la Maîtrise de l'Energie.

FIFTEEN

Apple Versus Google, Season One

Mobile phones have swamped the planet. There are now more than half a billion iPhones and over 2 billion phones running Android, the operating system developed by Google. Each platform supports more than a million downloadable applications, ranging from the most popular such as Facebook, YouTube or Whatsapp to others verging on the absurd, only of any use if you need a virtual lighter for a rock concert, a digital bottle opener or want to pop bubble wrap to relax. What competitive mechanisms and forces are at work behind this gigantic undertaking? In the next two chapters we shall suggest some leads, drawing on a series of economic concepts.

General-Purpose Technology, or the Path to Universal Adoption

The smartphone is a general-purpose technology.[1] Much as electricity or cars, this digital Swiss knife is transforming whole swathes of the economy. Widely available, a large number of industries have adopted it, despite it often sawing the branch on which they are sitting. Furthermore, it is fed by a steady stream of innovation which enhances performance and cuts costs. We don't even notice these characteristics any longer, because although smartphones have only existed for about ten years, they have become completely commonplace. Nor do we notice that we ourselves have become focused on our often-intense use of phono sapiens. Eight out of ten of us check our phone less than a quarter of an hour after waking up. Collectively, we take about 100 million selfies and assorted snaps a day.

Smartphones are increasingly universal.[2] Nearly one in three people in the world has one, or one in two if we only consider people aged over 16. In 2017, we purchased about 1.5 billion handsets.

Such global success gives innovators rapid access to a potential customer base all over the world. Think of Uber, now operating in more than 500 cities, Instagram or Snapchat, with their hundreds of millions of users exchanging pictures and videos, or even Rovio, the Finnish software firm that designed Angry Birds, downloaded 2 billion times. To this list of companies which happily do without the Internet and personal computers, we should also add those which have migrated their business to mobile phones, firms such as Dailymotion, Booking.com or LinkedIn. In all three cases the traffic generated by smartphones now outstrips access by PCs. This is hardly surprising given that the formers' installed base is twice the size. The world increasingly hinges on smartphones, less and less on computers.

Complementary Innovation, or How to Take Advantage of an Innovative Neighbour

The comparison between the smartphone with its many functions – camera, computer, alarm, compass, means of communication and such – and the Swiss army knife is not only valid for consumers. It is also a remarkable resource for innovative entrepreneurs. It offers inventors of applications and new services a host of complementary tools: secure payment system, calculator, data storage, global positioning, accelerometer, etc.[3] So inventors can take advantage of innovations that are already built-in, with no need to design or fund them. What's more, there are all the tools that the phone uses directly, typically connection to WiFi and Bluetooth networks and the Cloud. They too are the focus of constant innovation. To cite but a single example, the central processing unit on the iPhone 6 contains almost a thousand times more transistors that the Intel Pentium launched in 1993.

In short, the smartphone is a sort of global infrastructure which has substantially reduced the cost of innovation in the service industry, all the way through from research and development to market access.

Network Effects in Multi-Sided Platform Markets

The operating system may be seen as the engine of a smartphone and there are currently only two serious contenders. iOS runs on all Apple iPhones, whereas Android powers almost all other devices. In third position, Microsoft's Windows Mobile only accounts for 3% of the market. But why is the market dominated by two systems, and not just one? After all, in many markets based on digital technology – just think of the Google search engine – a single firm holds sway. Why not more than two, for that matter? What became of the Nokia and Blackberry systems?

The hegemonic position of a single company is the outcome of one of the simplest economic models used to analyse platforms, which connect the two sides of a market – in the present case the users of an operating system, on the one hand, and application developers, on the other.[4] The particularity of this connection is that for each side of the market the attractiveness of the platform depends on what happens on the other side. The more people there are using the operating system, the more developers stand to gain by developing applications to run on it. Conversely the more apps there are compatible with a particular system, the more attractive it is to users. Boosted by these mutually beneficial effects, the platform expands, like a snowball rolling down a slope. Developers and users cluster round the platform which becomes a monopoly.

When a Market Tips in Favour of a Single Firm

In practice, it is a bit more complicated: far from starting at the top of the slope, the snowball originates at the bottom. So it needs to be pushed uphill first to set it in motion. The diagram below explains this idea. The hill-shaped curve represents demand for the platform, or in other words, willingness to pay as a function of the number of users. On the left we have the early adopters – for example, the people who will queue all night outside a shop in order to be the first to buy a new phone. From their point of view, the coveted good has a high intrinsic value, so they are prepared to buy it despite it only having been adopted by a tiny proportion of the population. On the right, on the contrary, are consumers who will only take the plunge once the good has been largely adopted by others. The horizontal dotted line plots the price of the good.

So why is it necessary to start by pushing the snowball up the slope? Simply because, even the most hard-line geeks would not buy

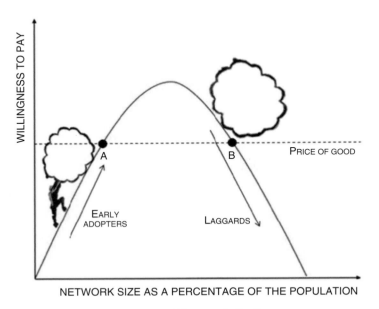

Figure 15.1: The snowball effect

the good, there being too few other users. In the present case, pushing the snowball uphill means subsidizing early purchasers. But the market tips in its favour once it has passed point A.[5] The snowball climbs and increases in size all on its own, passing the top and rushing on down the other side, becoming huge in the process, until it reaches point B, where it grinds to a halt. It stops because the remaining consumers attach so little intrinsic value to the platform that it does not interest them, despite having been adopted by almost all the others.

The Perils of Backing the Wrong Technological Horse

At the end of the 2000s, Google and Nokia were each pushing their snowball up the hill and Google won. Yet Nokia started with the advantage of having pioneered smartphones, thanks in particular to its Symbian operating system. There were 10,000 applications running under the system before Google entered the game. But the Mountain View firm caught up with its Finnish competitor and reached the tipping point first. Nine months after Android launched, 30,000 apps were available for smartphones running this operating system. Despite enjoying a comfortable initial lead, Nokia took several years to achieve a number three times lower.

The time taken to reach the tipping point depends on the price and quality of the good, and on subsidies for early adopters. But there are other factors. Consumer expectations also play a key part. It is best to avoid adopting the losing platform: you would find yourself with a product or service that will be gradually sidelined, with declining use-value.[6] Think of all the people who loyally stuck with Blackberry or Nokia smartphones. In the end, they had to resign themselves to switching to Apple iPhones, or Samsung or LG devices running Android. They may well have lost documents and music, stored in formats that are no longer supported, not to mention their personal set-up. They also had to figure out a new system, and so on. If a winner is picked, by users around you, by the trade and media, you would be well advised to follow suit, even if personally you prefer another platform. If you are in business, try to influence the general public and opinion-makers, for convictions about the future winner tend to be self-fulfilling.

But this doesn't explain why Android and iOS are still in the running and why this situation is likely to last.[7] Two words sum up the answer provided by economic analysis of platforms: differentiation and multi-homing.[8] But to explain them we shall need a second set of economic concepts, or in other words you will have to read the next chapter!

Notes

1. Evans, D. and Schmalensee, R. (2016), *Matchmakers: The New Economics of Multisided Platforms*, Boston, MA: Harvard Business Review Press.
2. 'Planet of the phones. The smartphone is ubiquitous, addictive and transformative', *The Economist*, 26 February 2015.
3. Scotchmer, S. (2004), *Innovation and Incentives*, Cambridge, MA: MIT Press.
4. Evans and Schmalensee, *Matchmakers*, ibid.
5. Katz, M. and Shapiro, C. (1994), 'Systems competition and network effects', *The Journal of Economic Perspectives*, 8(2): 93–115.
6. Ibid.
7. Bresnahan, T., Orsini, J. and Yin, P-L. (2014), 'Platform choice by mobile-app developers', Institute for Economic Policy Research, Stanford University.
8. Ibid.

SIXTEEN

Apple Versus Google, Season Two

Google and Apple dominate the world of smartphones, thanks respectively to their Android and iOS operating systems. Yet they are not locked in face-to-face competition, being rooted in quite different business ecosystems and models. More importantly, their platforms are differentiated, even if they support the same killer apps, from Angry Birds to YouTube, through Facebook and Uber. This explains why rivalry between the two West Coast firms is likely to last, without one necessarily sidelining the other. But if we turn our attention to the countless application developers, competition is head-on and ferocious. They are all intent on drawing and holding the attention of consumers. They are also in competition with Google, which pre-installs its proprietary apps (Google Earth, Finance, Weather, Maps, Search, etc.). This practice is the focus of criticism by competition authorities. Let's take a closer look at all this, drawing on a new set of economic concepts.

Business Model, or How to Deliver Customer Value and Convert It into Profits

The iPhone, which was launched in 2007, is consistent with Apple's strategy of integrating soft and hardware. iOS is neither licensed nor sold separately. Much the same applies to the App Store. Apps are bundled with the handset, from which Apple derives most of its mobile-related revenue.[1] The iPhone is only open to app developers and telecommunications operators, yet even this opening is subject to conditions. Apple develops and owns proprietary apps. They are already installed on the phone at the time of purchase and they cannot be deleted, or at least with great difficulty. Some, such as Photo or Safari, contribute to the value of the phone, without generating revenue. Others, such as iTunes, do, thanks to downloads purchased by users.

In addition, when Apple rolled out its smartphone, it signed exclusive agreements with only one operator in each country, limiting access to the latter's customers and requiring the operator to subsidize iPhone sales.[2] At the outset, Apple succeeded in finding an operator in every target market prepared to accept its drastic terms, because the phone, with its big, touch-screen, user-friendly interface, handy design and apps, seemed to be the epitome of a smartphone, despatching precursors such as Blackberry or Nokia to the dustbin of history.[3]

Business Ecosystem, or the Interplay of Collaboration and Complementarity

In contrast, the Google ecosystem, which is based on Android and its application store Google Play, is open and free of charge. A few months after the iPhone launch, a consortium headed by Google and comprising telecommunications operators, handset manufacturers and software developers announced the arrival of phones running Android. They formed a sort of united front in opposition to Apple, a newcomer to the phone business which had proved an immediate success. Google's accommodating attitude encouraged large numbers of manufacturers and operators hurriedly to adopt Android. It not only gave them access to the user interface and source code, but also made no charge for the licence. It even passed on a share of advertising revenue derived from its search engine. On the other hand, with Google Play, manufacturers and operators had to accept a whole series of proprietary Google apps, which had to be pre-installed and were inseparable from Google Play. Theoretically, manufacturers can develop their own version of Android, but in that case they can no longer install Google Play and lose a share of advertising revenue.

Android is a sort of Trojan horse which has found its way into 80% of the world's smartphones. It has enabled Google to migrate its software from PCs to mobile devices and in so doing extend its publicity-related business. This holds true for its search engine, but also for other high-profile apps such as YouTube. Google has thus adapted its way of working to a two-tiered substitution process.[4] First, the pairs of eyes and mouse clicks of such importance to organizations purchasing publicity are shifting their focus from PCs to smartphones. At the same time, their volume is growing much faster on smartphones. In a similar vein, smartphones make data gathering much easier, enabling consumers' movements to be tracked thanks to the device in their pocket. Second, smartphone users tend to make more use of apps to access services (weather forecast, hotel booking, etc.) directly rather than via the search engine, previously Google's prime source of publicity revenue.

Differentiation, When Products Are No Longer Quite the Same

Android and iOS are differentiated platforms. Apple exclusively targets the upper end of the market, where Android phones also target medium and lower segments. So the average iPhone user is more prosperous. In the United States, the median user of Apple phones earns 40% more than their Android counterpart. A larger proportion of the population of developing countries uses an Android phone. We should point out in passing that the fact that Google's operating system and apps are free has been one of the key factors enabling the unit price of smartphones to drop below $50.

The owners of iPhones also spend more time browsing or phoning, and are more inclined to purchase additional apps. Consumers download far more applications from Google Play than from App Store, but the value of the latter's sales is twice as high.

Multi-Homing: Developing Competition Between Platforms

The vast majority of firms developing smartphone apps target only one platform. They design the software for sale by one or other outlet. The cost of writing software for a specific platform explains why they opt for single-homing. The code in part of an application will need to be changed for it to work under iOS or Android. Making an app compatible with both operating systems doubles its price. Choosing one or the other depends on the type of consumer a firm is targeting, in terms of geography and sociology. On the other hand, it has little to do with the terms in the contract, which are similar. Developers must pay a registration fee of under $100, then pay Apple or Google 30% of revenue from downloads of paid apps and from purchases made using the apps (buying lives or weapons for characters in games, for example).

On the other hand, multi-homing is de rigueur for apps that aim to achieve or have already achieved massive success, and for Web 2.0 or 'social' apps.[5] From the outset, leading developers of games or services write their software for both platforms. The same applies to companies, such as banks, airlines or couriers which interact with their customers. If an app designed for one platform attracts a large number of users as soon as it launches, it will immediately be ported to the other platform.

Of the 2 million apps available on each platform, only a very small number can be found on both App Store and Google Play. But in strictly business terms, multi-homing is the dominant trend, quite simply because on the whole we are all interested in the same apps.

Just twenty of them account for 80% of all downloaded apps.[6] No mistake! We really mean twenty apps and not 20% of all apps. In other words, there is no need for consumers to opt for iOS or Android to use a specific app. Regardless of which smartphone you own, you can access Facebook, YouTube, Uber, TripAdvisor, Angry Birds, Instagram and Shazam, big banks, national rail operators and such. Alongside them you will find a myriad others catering for niche audiences, among which you will no doubt find just what you want. So as both platforms offer the same services there is every reason for their co-existence to continue.

When Apparent Economic Abundance Conceals Scarcity

The average user does not install many apps – thirty or so in the USA and France. They only use a much smaller number in a regular way, for two, separate reasons. They lack the time needed to find more apps, download them and learn how they work. They lack sufficient room on their phone too, with its cluttered display and saturated storage. So space is at a premium, all the more so because the visibility of apps depends on rankings, such as the week's 10 most popular games or the month's 20 most popular cooking apps. To stand a chance of getting onto one of these lists, contenders must spend huge amounts on marketing and publicity, particularly on social media.

The world of mobile apps has become ultracompetitive. Developers must vie with dozens of similar products and hundreds of others of the same type (games to develop toddlers' motor skills, how best to match food and wine, etc.). But above all they must cope with a much larger number of totally unrelated apps, also out to catch the attention of prospective users.

There might be apps of interest to you among the millions of apps with a small or perhaps non-existent audience, but it is akin to finding a needle in a haystack. There is no effective tool for tracking down just the right app, nothing like the Internet search engines which seamlessly connect individual queries with a stupendous mass of data. So it is an upward struggle to make full use of the many apps that only interest a few people.

Tying to Make Two Products Inseparable

Competition authorities on both sides of the Atlantic are concerned about Android's hegemony. In Russia, the Federal Antimonopoly Service found that Google had 'violated antimonopoly legislation in part of abuse of its dominant position'. The European Commission has fined Google €4.3 billion and the US Federal Trade Commission has started an inquiry.[7] The concern is that Google may be forcing phone manufacturers, wishing to gain access to Android and Google Play, to pre-install proprietary apps.

Google's licensing contracts tie use of the Android operating system and Google Play to installation of other apps such as Google Search, Chrome and YouTube.[8] In so doing, the Mountain View colossus is allegedly preventing phone manufacturers from choosing similar, rival apps, or developing their own set of apps and installing them as they choose on their phones. So the thrust of this claim is that manufacturers can differentiate their handsets with regard to technical performance and innovative design, but they cannot do the same with their apps. Unless of course they agree to do without the almost inevitable suite of Google apps.

This case is reminiscent of the conduct remedies and fine the European Commission imposed on Microsoft. Brussels concluded that the firm had broken EU competition law by tying proprietary Media Player software to its Windows operating system, a practice that obstructed competitors. It was quite possible to buy a PC and subsequently download other media players, but their developers had little chance of winning over a PC user base equivalent to Microsoft's. The applications tied to Windows benefited de facto from the system's omnipresence on PCs worldwide. Furthermore, when consumers buy a new machine they tend not to tweak the default setup. Only if they have much higher expectations of a competing product's performance will consumers remove pre-installed software. Otherwise, there would be little incentive to waste time finding out about the price and features of possible substitutes then downloading them. Under these conditions, it is an uphill struggle for Dailymotion to compete with YouTube, which is pre-installed on 80% of the world's smartphones, excepting in China. This is because the Chinese authorities have outlawed Google Play and many of Google's proprietary apps. Phone manufacturers have developed various versions of Android, taking advantage of it being open software. Competition and innovation in apps seems to be stronger there, offering consumers more choice. But there is a downside: the diversity and fragmentation of operating systems and apps reduces the size of platforms and entails compatibility problems.

In a few years, after the decisions of the Court of First Instance and the European Court of Justice in Luxembourg, in the event of two appeals, we shall find out whether the EU thinks Google's tied apps jeopardize consumer interests.

In the meantime, the focus of competition will probably have shifted. Innovation gallops on, whereas anti-trust law primarily disciplines past behaviour. At present there is an app for everything and everyone, even if we don't know how to find them. The app business is mature. By the time the various authorities have issued their rulings on Android, competition may have moved to chatbots. In case you're not familiar with this concept, a chatbot gets round the need for apps, talking to users to answer messages addressed to them. It can, for instance, book a flight, set up a meeting or order a take-away meal. Facebook and Microsoft have apparently got a head start in this field, which depends on artificial intelligence.

Soon there may be a chatbot to answer all your questions on economic analysis of competition!

Notes

1. Teece, D. (2010), 'Business models, business strategy and innovation', *Long Range Planning*, 43: 172–194.
2. Winter, J. (2014), 'Success factors of mobile business ecosystems. From hardware-centric to content and advertising-based business models', Licentiate Thesis, Department of Computer Science and Engineering, Helsinki, Finland.
3. Ibid.
4. Moore, J. (2006), 'Business ecosystems and the view from the firm', *Antitrust Bulletin*, 51(1): 31–75.
5. Gabszewicz, J. and Wauthy, X. (2005), 'Two-sided markets and price competition with multi-homing', Université Catholique de Louvain, Core discussion paper 2004030.
6. Bresnahan, T., Orsini, J. and Yin, P-L. (2014), 'Platform choice by mobile-app developers', Institute for Economic Policy Research, Stanford University.
7. Antitrust: Commission fines Google € 4.34 billion for illegal practices regarding Android. European Commission Press Release, 18 July 2018.
8. Blume, L. and Durlauf, S. (ed.) (2008), 'Bundling and tying', in *The New Palgrave Dictionary of Economics*, New York, NY: Palgrave Macmillan.

SEVENTEEN

Super Mario Can Die, but like Nintendo, He Has Several Lives

Super Mario, the little plumber with a moustache, is well into his thirties, after making a big contribution to Nintendo's enduring success. Unlike its competitors, the Kyoto-based firm has been a player in the home video-game console market since the early days. This is quite an achievement, many having perished on the way, including companies such as Atari or Sega which once dominated the market. To survive in this industry one needs lots of superpowers, including the ability to set prices.

Short, Brutish Cycles

You've certainly heard of Microsoft and its Xbox, Sony and its PlayStation, but what about Fairchild, Coleco or 3DO? Probably not, unless you're a hardened old-timer, familiar with all seven generations that preceded contemporary consoles.

The video-game industry is subject to short cycles, one technology driving out the previous one, with a succession of new entrants and failed leavers. No one stays in the lead for long. Current sales are dominated by Nintendo's Switch console, the PlayStation 4 and Xbox One. The three unknowns belonging to earlier generations fell into the dungeon at the castle of Princess Peach, whom Super Mario must save on Level 24.

In 1976, Fairchild rolled out its first console with a separate game cartridge. Prior to that, Atari and several other manufacturers had sold machines with games built-in, which limited their number. Drastically so in the early days: you could only play Pong on Atari's first home video console. Imagine a black screen with a white dot moving back and forth, from left to right then back again, with two vertical white lines going up and down, controlled by a knob. What was supposed to represent a game of ping-pong bears no comparison with today's breathtakingly realistic sports contests.

Coleco entered the market four years later and soon took the lead in sales thanks to its exclusive licence for Donkey Kong in the United States, a game in which Mario made his first appearance along with a rather dumb gorilla. In 1994, 3DO became the first company to market a console with a 32-bit processor. Unlike its competitors, it had decided not to manufacture anything in-house, neither hardware nor games software, contracting all this work out to partners operating under licence.

Temporary Monopolies

Fairchild, Coleco and 3DO are just three examples among many others. We chose them as illustrations of how tough competition is. The console games industry is emblematic of the dynamic competition model in which the first entrant, or first vendor – often the same thing – does not benefit for long from their temporary monopoly. Consumers can count on the speed of technological innovation and market virtue, with no fear of a single company achieving limitless domination. The Coloco console's reign only lasted five years, which corresponds to the average length of each console generation so far. The first entrants, Fairchild and 3DO, only survived for one cycle. More successful ventures such as Atari and Sega only held on for three cycles. In contrast, Nintendo has been operating since the very beginning; later entrants Microsoft and Sony are still active too.[1]

The reasons why some survive and others do not depend on various factors, first the quality of consoles, particularly regarding graphics and performance. It is preferable not to miss a rung on the technology ladder, sticking too long to an outdated format, such as a 64-bit processor instead of a 128-bit chip, or cartridges instead of CD-Roms.

A second key factor is the variety and quality of the games on offer when a console launches, or is expected to follow. With no games, a console is useless to consumers. Similarly a console that no one buys is of no value to games developers. This may seem reminiscent of the network effects essential to platform economics (see Chapter 15): the larger the user base, the more attractive the platform will be to developers; the greater the number of developers, the more attractive it will be to users.

3DO failed because too few games were developed for its console. Unlike its competitors, it could not fall back on in-house development of games to prime early sales of its system, until such time as third-party publishers could deliver their software.

Obviously, the quality of games matters too. Nintendo pulled off a succession of product launches with only a small number of games, but they were all excellent. Two-thirds of the world's bestsellers are Nintendo games.[2]

Third, the size of the installed base is very important. The success of Sony consoles is due, at least in part, to scope for playing some of the old games on the next model. With backward compatibility, it has managed to roll out a new console with a huge choice of games. In this way it reduces the risk of existing customers switching to rival consoles.

Fourth, the survival and success of game companies depends on the decisions they take on pricing. This dimension deserves more detailed analysis, for it reflects and impacts on some of the preceding factors.

The Infernal Game of Setting Prices

We should start by pointing out that games and video consoles belong to the durable-goods category. Consumers may buy them when they first come out or much later. Ronald Coase, winner of the Nobel prize for economics in 1991, demonstrated that for this sort of good a monopoly competes with itself.[3] Accordingly, it sets its price at marginal cost, without making any profit despite its hegemonic position.

The explanation for this apparent paradox is consumer anticipation. They expect the price of the good to fall as time passes. Having sold it to the first buyers at the monopoly price, it seems likely that the firm would be tempted to lower the price slightly in order to sell the product to other buyers, only inclined to purchase it when it is slightly cheaper. This done, the firm would again be tempted to drop its price again, and so on. But having foreseen this trend, potential buyers would delay their purchase until such time as the monopolist had nothing to gain by reducing its price, in other words when it had reached a price equal to its marginal cost. Below that level the firm would lose money.

Only if consumer preferences diverge can a company find a way out of this diabolical trap. Some want the good there and then for their immediate gratification, others are more patient. In this case, the seller can apply different prices over time. A high launch price skims off the market segment comprising consumers with the greatest willingness to pay, followed by a slightly lower price for the next segment and so on. A classic example of this approach is books, initially published in hardback, then in paperback a while later. In the jargon of economic theory this is known as inter-temporal differentiation.

Time after time we have seen the price of the same console model or game gradually drop. For example, the Xbox and PS2 each went through four price cuts during the first few years of their existence.[4] Similarly, the price of Ubisoft's Monaco Grand Prix game was reduced five times in the six months following its launch.[5]

Of course, these drops are partly due to decisions by the competition. Unlike the monopoly considered by Coase, video-game companies may see their skimming schemes upset by the pricing strategies of rival firms.

Another difficulty relates to the negative impact of a high launch price on a console's market penetration. To take full advantage of the snowball effect (see Chapter 15) of network economics, it is in the interests of a console manufacturer for a new product to be adopted quickly; this is an incentive to set a low launch price. So, when setting their price, they have no option but to make allowance for both contrary effects on their profit stream over time.

We should also point out that by separating the game medium from its console, Fairchild introduced a real headache: the price to set for the console, on the one hand, and for the software, on the other, given that they are complementary. Prior to this move, things were simple, there being just one price for the whole system.

Setting the Price of Consoles and Games

Just for a second, put yourself in the shoes of Tatsumi Kimishima, president of Nintendo. Given that you will be spending 100 to develop, manufacture and market a new console, how are you to recoup that outlay? You could sell the console for 10 and recoup the rest from your own games and from sales commissions on others designed by third-party firms. Or sell the console for 90 and recoup the remaining 10 on games. Or split the costs 50–50.

Almost without exception, the industry has taken the first option, sometimes going to even greater extremes. Microsoft pitched the price of the Xbox 360 so low it lost over $100 on every console it sold; Sony did the same with the PS3.[6]

This is obviously a risky strategy. If game sales do not live up to expectations, it may mean massive losses. Sega dominated the market for two generations with very popular consoles. But it had to pull out of the game due to inadequate revenue from sales of software. It did not make up for the half a billion dollars or so that the subsidy for the Dreamcast cost.[7] At first sight, you might think 3DO had adopted a safer course of action when it set the price of its console at

$699, three times higher than competing systems. But the device did not sell and, despite the very low sales commissions charged by 3DO, developers were in no hurry to design games for it. Competition makes it very difficult to disregard a pricing model that gives priority to one or other side of the market.

Pricing Headaches

You may think it goes without saying that pricing should be skewed in favour of low-cost consoles. Surely it makes sense to start the snowball rolling with new models penetrating the market fast. But this overlooks the conflicting merits of preliminary skimming of eager early adopters. Moreover, the lower the price of the console, the less the seller locks in consumers purchasing it. They will be less inclined to switch to another one if their console cost $500, rather than half as much. Lastly, the snowball can start from the other side of the hill (see Chapter 15), by luring developers in with low sales commissions. This in turn ensures there will be a plentiful supply of games, making the console more attractive, so that ultimately it can be sold for more. In short, allowance must be made for the strength of network effects and demand elasticity: how many more purchasers does a cheaper console yield? Incidentally, how many more games? After all, developers will focus primarily on the consoles most likely to be popular. Lastly, how many more games does a lower commission generate, and hence how many more consumers buy a console?

With video-game consoles, as for any other two-sided market, allowance must be made for a host of effects pushing in various directions. So setting the optimal price is a real headache, despite recent advances in economic theory in this field, building on the pioneering work of Jean Tirole, winner of the Nobel prize for economics in 2014.[8]

Competition is one of the factors driving the dominant pricing model in the video-game industry. This intuitive explanation was proposed by an economist at Harvard Business School, drawing on a model that is both sophisticated and original.[9] Assuming that consumer preferences vary with regard to games, third-party developers are protected by the lower substitutability of their game and consequently achieve higher margins. Knowing this, it is in the interests of the console manufacturer to charge third-party developers higher sales commissions, which in turn means the hardware can be cheaper.

Nintendo Resurgent

In 2016, Nintendo, the only pioneering home-video console manufacturer to have survived, was in a bad way. Its most recent product, the WiiU, was a commercial fiasco, selling little more than 20 million units worldwide in five years, less than its predecessor, the Wii. Unlike its main competitors, Nintendo had not diversified outside consoles in preparation for such shocks. So it struggled to weather the storm. Furthermore, Nintendo had still not started to adapt its games to play on smartphones and tablets, despite the fact that games on these platforms were a severe threat to its position. They appealed mostly to occasional players, precisely the consumers who made up its core customer base. It is important to note that Pokémon Go, downloaded half a billion times in summer 2016, was not developed by Nintendo itself, but by a US firm working under licence. Only six months later did Nintendo launch Super Mario Run, the first game for mobile devices developed in-house. The free version was a success, but not the version costing just under $10, which was too high a price.

The following year, Nintendo staked its future on the Switch, a hybrid console that worked equally well at home and on-the-go. At its pre-launch, presentation games specialists were dubious. Their forecasts for the success of this innovative model were gloomy. But they were wrong. In 2017, the Switch ousted Sony's PS4 to take first place in the global ranking, selling more than 10 million units. Nintendo lived to fight another day, spared the fate of another Japanese firm, Sega, which after dropping out of the console market, now only develops gaming software.

Much as its valiant plumber hero, Nintendo overcame countless obstacles to pick up lots of gold coins, earning it new lives for games to come.

Notes

1. Gallagher, S. and Park, S. H. (2002), 'Innovation and competition in standard-based industries: a historical analysis of the US home video game market', IEEE Xplore Digital Library.
2. Davidovici-Nora, M. and Bourreau, M. (2012), 'Les marchés à deux versants dans l'industrie des jeux vidéo', *Réseaux*, 173–174(3): 97–135.
3. Coase, R. H. (1972), 'Durability and Monopoly', *The Journal of Law & Economics*, 15(1): 143–149.
4. Davidovici-Nora and Bourreau, 'Les marchés à deux versants dans l'industrie des jeux vidéo', ibid.
5. Nair, H. S. (2006), 'Intertemporal price discrimination with forward-looking consumers: application to the US market for console video-games', Stanford Graduate School of Business working paper 1947.
6. Davidovici-Nora, M. and Bourreau, M. (2012), 'Les marchés à deux versants dans l'industrie des jeux vidéo', ibid.
7. 'Cast aside', *The Economist*, 25 January 2001.
8. Rochet, J.-C. and Tirole, J. (2003), 'Platform competition in two-sided markets', *Journal of the European Economic Association*, 1(4): 990–1029.
9. Hagiu, A. (2009), 'Two-sided platforms: product variety and pricing structures', *Journal of Economics & Management Strategy*, 18: 1011–1043.

EIGHTEEN

Intermezzo, on a Theme of Disruptive Innovation

It is immediately apparent that the pace of innovation has speeded up, particularly if we look at how the Internet has developed. Just think back to the 1990s. In the middle of the decade there were only some tens of thousands of users. The first bestseller on the digital economy was published at this point.[1] Since then, the number of Internet users and publications has soared. However, it would be more relevant to our inquiry to take the 1980s as the moment when innovation started to gather speed, for by then development of information and communications technology was already underway. Microsoft started life in 1973, with Apple following three years later. They now rank among the oldest firms to have based their growth on these technologies. In company with Google they represent the world's top three firms in terms of market value.

By putting the moment when the pace of innovation started to accelerate before the Internet boom, we can avoid the pitfall of over-playing its importance and focusing exclusively on forms of competition linked to it, particularly in retailing, but also the success of the Silicon Valley giants. It would be a mistake to overlook the rapid growth of other business models that have nothing to do with the digital economy. The Swedish firm Ikea, for instance, opened its first shop outside Scandinavia in 1973, in Switzerland. Over the next twenty years, the number of its shops worldwide rose from nine to 114.[2]

It is immediately apparent, to all and sundry, that the gathering pace of innovation creates novelty and destroys old empires, at one and the same time. We have grown quite used to endless talk of disruption and uberization. Nearly 60 years ago, Joseph Schumpeter wrote of 'creative destruction', a term that is just as evocative and probably more meaningful. He was the first economist to acknowledge that innovation was key to competition. Competition no longer went hand-in-hand with a market defined by the high or low number of its buyers and sellers, rather it was part-and-parcel with the disruptive innovation in which an entrepreneur engages.

Schumpeter's View of Innovation and Competition

A soothsayer is said to have glanced into the cradle of Joseph Alois Schumpeter shortly after his birth. That was in 1883, the same year as John Maynard Keynes was born, but also the year Karl Marx died. Much as Schumpeter, both authors tried in their way to make sense of capitalism. The diviner predicted that the infant would grow up to be the greatest lover in Vienna, the best horseman in Europe, and the greatest economist in the world. Allegedly, Schumpeter bragged that he had only failed to achieve one of these goals but did not say which. His enemies, familiar with him in one of these three fields, added that it must have been in the other two that the soothsayer's prophecy had come true . . .

He was probably thinking of the third prediction. A doctor of law, banker and finance minister, he only gave his full attention to his career as a professor of economics on reaching Harvard, in his early forties. Following neither Keynes nor the neo-classical school, he was never seen by his peers as the greatest economist of his time. But he was the first to take an interest in innovation and dynamic competition. Indeed some of his original thinking is still valid.

First, innovation is not restricted to technical matters. Designing a new product or service using existing technology while inventing a new business model or organization certainly counts as innovation. In some cases, the effects may be more far-reaching than new technology. Dollar Shave Club is a case in point, combining strands from Amazon and Netflix and applying them to razors (see Chapter 13). Moreover, innovation goes much further than invention because it includes all the stages between research and market launch. Whereas an invention must stand a chance of finding an application or use, for example, in order to obtain a patent, innovation must be applied on a large scale in real life. So development of a new product cannot be treated as innovative until it has reached the market.

In addition, an innovator is not necessarily, indeed rarely, a researcher, unless of course the latter is also, or turns into, an entrepreneur. The key figure in innovation is the entrepreneur, orchestrating innovation by combining all the factors needed for it to happen, be they scientific, financial or commercial. John D. Rockefeller (Standard Oil), George Eastman (Kodak) or Thomas Edison (General Electric), all contemporaries of Schumpeter, are some of the prime instances of this model. Were he still alive, the Harvard economist would no doubt be looking at such as Bill Gates (Microsoft), Jeff Bezos (Amazon) or, to stray outside the United States, Ingvar Kamprad (Ikea). Not to mention the tens of thousands of people all over the world who have launched start-ups.

His second idea was that competition by innovation makes ordinary competition negligible. In the comparison cited on the opening page of this part, Schumpeter likens the first to bombardment, whereas the latter is no more dramatic than 'forcing a door'.

Competition on prices, capacity or even quality takes second place for several reasons. Unlike competition by innovation, it is too feeble to drive economic growth on its own. The disproportionate relation between the two forces is also visible in their effects. Competition by innovation sidelines a large number of companies and whole swathes of industry. It may even lead to their complete disappearance, witness Blackberry and its personal assistants banished from the market by smartphones. In contrast, competition which makes do with forcing doors leads to only minor shifts in market share between established companies while affording limited access to new entrants. On account of its powerful macro and microeconomic effects, competition by innovation requires the keenest attention of economists. Schumpeter castigated his fellows for looking the wrong way. They spent their time studying the imperfections of competition in a static world, instead of trying to remedy the shortcomings holding back dynamic competition. There would be less basis for such criticism now, many economists having taken an interest in competition by innovation. As we have seen in the preceding chapters, it is more accurately described and modelled nowadays.

Schumpeter's third idea was that large firms which enjoy monopoly power – consequently registering excess profit – are in the best position to innovate. This claim is the most controversial, even today, despite thousands of research papers on the topic. Yet in theoretical terms, the question is easily stated: is a market structure based on monopoly or on perfect competition most favourable to innovation? Or stated more empirically: do we see more innovation in markets in which concentration is high, or in those where it is low? In both cases, it is difficult to provide an answer, because the connection between concentration or monopoly power, on the one hand, and innovation, on the other, operates in both directions. In simple terms, before innovation starts, the market structure (in other words the number of market players) determines the amount of profit and by extension the capacity of companies to invest in innovation. But once innovation kicks in, its success generates a new market structure: the successful innovator's market share will increase, competitors will be sidelined, and the innovator's profits will rise. The companies obviously anticipate this market power, which acts ex ante on their decision to innovate. Achieving a dominant position, or better still a monopoly, is a powerful stimulus to find new products and business models. In short, the incentives to innovate depend on the difference between the size of the company before and after innovation, which in turn depends on the market structure before and after. We should note in passing that Schumpeter thought that carrying out research and subsequently achieving competitive advantage were part of a continuous back-and-forth movement. Innovation, he believed, much as patents which have only limited shelf life, only delivers a temporary monopoly. The innovator who one day overtakes the competition will inevitably end up by being sidelined or even eliminated altogether, marking the start of a new cycle.

The diversity of innovations and forms of competition is a further source of complexity. The correlation between competition and innovation may switch from positive to negative, or the opposite, depending on whether or not it is easy to imitate an innovation, or whether stiffer competition means less product differentiation or less concentration.[3] In addition other factors, such as ease of access to complementary innovations, the presence of network effects or the availability of a robust venture-capital industry, also alter the scope and incentives for innovation according to the size of the company. Lastly, as an emeritus professor at the University of California at Berkeley pointed out, the problem is not that we lack a model of the connection between innovation and competition, rather that there are so many.[4] So it is hard to know which one suits the context of the market we are studying.

Disruption and Uberization

In the discussion above, we have used the term 'innovation' in its narrow, disruptive sense. But we may broaden that definition to include the gradual innovation that companies achieve in their day-to-day existence, or almost. After all, a company must constantly improve what already exists, do better at what it already knows how to do, achieving lower costs, a more efficient organization, higher R&D productivity, better product quality and customer service, among others. Static competition demands such efforts. Companies are all competing in a sort of long-distance run, on a clearly sign-posted course and subject to set rules. They may run at varying speeds, move up or down the ranking, but if they stop running they will be disqualified.

It may seem a contradiction in terms to connect a race to a static state, but in fact companies need to race to keep up with the others and stay in the same place, just as the Red Queen pointed out to Alice in Lewis Carroll's *Through the Looking Glass*. Biologists have taken up this image to describe competition between species and the constant adaptation it imposes on living beings. Corporate strategy analysts use the same metaphor in reference to the need for organizations continuously to adapt.[5]

But what characterizes the world today is not so much companies running on the spot, rather their attempts to steer an even course through a hurricane of creative destruction. Two new words have appeared to describe how they weather the storm, or not: disruption and uberization. They have become largely interchangeable, their meaning having evolved. Uberization has above all been used to qualify disruptive innovation linked to information technology, particularly platforms such as Amazon, Airbnb and of course Uber, which bypass conventional means of purchasing goods and services. In the two chapters on smartphones and their applications, we looked at the main concepts and competition models which these technologies have upset. For a long time, disruption had a very specific meaning, popularized by Clayton M. Christensen, a professor at Harvard Business School, namely disruptive innovations that initially give rise to products delivering mediocre performance. Let's take a closer look at this bottom-up uberization, because competition takes form and develops here in an original way.

To begin with, disruptive innovation is only interested in customers who have been sidelined or completely ignored. For example, long-distance car-pooling initially targeted young people who lacked the means to take the train and only made their minds up at the last minute. The products or services delivered by disruptive innovation have one or more features which appeal to a small number of consumers – low-cost travel without advance booking, in the present case. Their performance with respect to other criteria – the ones that most consumers demand and value – is disappointing, witness the long journey times, scant comfort and little privacy associated with car-sharing.

Let's look at another example, for the over-30s among our readers: pinball! However hard you tried to keep the ball in play, the machine always ended up swallowing it. You could shake the table, more or less vigorously, to correct the trajectory, trying to hit the bumpers and flippers which would boost your score, winning extra balls and maybe a free game. These machines, with plenty of flashing lights, reached the peak of their popularity in the 1980s. About ten years earlier, the first arcade games with a screen had appeared alongside them, but at first sight they stood little chance of supplanting pinball. Indeed the first one was an object of scorn, a black screen with a white dot moving back and forth, from left to right, then back again, and two vertical white lines, controlled by the player, which could go up and down and were supposed to represent ping-pong bats. No flashing lights, just one, obsessive sound, and two knobs, one for each player, to control the bats: in short here was a game of very little interest in comparison to pinball. But it was a game with a screen like a TV, a game everyone, from kids to pensioners, could play, and much as pachinko (a cross between pinball and a one-armed bandit) in Japan, it had nothing to do with virility.[6] Pong terminals could be installed in fast-food eateries and shopping malls. Pong was followed by Pac-Man, a sort of gluttonous enzyme that swallowed dots in a maze haunted by ghosts, and by many other video games, in colour, on bigger screens and with higher definition, including brutal first-person shooters which finally appealed to dominant-male pinball players.

The game now seems totally outdated and only one manufacturer of pinball tables has survived in the USA. It caters exclusively for the nostalgia market. Arcade games have gradually vanished from cafes and similar venues, unable to compete with the consoles on which we can play at home, even taking on other (virtual) adversaries at the other end of an Internet connection. Gone too is all that cigarette smoke and drinks, but also the companionship of neighbours or schoolmates. Arcade games and then consoles have gradually taken over the market occupied by their old competitors, but above all they have vastly enlarged it. Every year Nintendo and its rivals sell tens of millions of home video consoles, whereas the annual record for pinball machines never topped 150,000.

Some consumers are sidelined because incumbents are obsessed with moving up-market, a seemingly sure way of achieving profit and growth: profit, because margins are higher up-market with more sophisticated products; growth, because middle and lower-income consumers end up adopting the same products, once they become more affordable or simply because no one manufactures or markets more straightforward, down-market goods any longer. Under these circumstances, why should incumbents take an interest in customers who only want straightforward, down-market goods?

Competition by innovators such as BlaBlaCar or Dollar Shave Club is consequently not initially perceived as a real threat. Indeed, they are not seen as potential competitors at all, unlike established companies operating in other geographic markets, which might decide to extend their business beyond their existing preserve. So incumbents pay no attention to such innovators and only respond when the upstarts improve their product or service sufficiently for it to vie with what is already on the market. Only by improving the performance of the features demanded by conventional customers can they hope to win over consumers loyal to the incumbents. But at that point they will also be better placed to poach new customers, enjoying an advantage in terms of price or quality over the incumbents' offering.

According to Christensen and many strategic management gurus, the alternatives available to incumbents are starkly blunt: uberize or be uberized, in other words innovate or die. If they carry on with the methods that secured their initial success, in particular giving priority to the customers they know best and who yield the greatest revenue, they are doomed. A newcomer, surfing on new technology, will invent a new business model and chase conventional companies out of the market.

However this maxim is certainly not valid in every case. First, an incumbent may resort to solutions other than engaging in disruptive innovation itself. The simplest response is to buy out – or form an alliance with – the firm behind the innovation that represents a threat. This solution is widespread, witness the many take-overs of start-ups of various sizes by large, well established technology firms such as Google or Facebook.

Second, there are other ways of innovating apart from targeting sidelined, down-market consumers. When Tesla entered the car industry, it started by competing with top-of-the-range models sold by incumbents. Similarly, the success of Apple's iPhone owes nothing to down-at-heel consumers or short-sighted, fat-fingered punters in need of a large touchscreen. Admittedly, smartphones were initially far inferior to PCs but their sales have eaten into and ultimately overtaken those of the once dominant devices.

Uncertainties

Uncertainty weighs heavily on Schumpeterian innovation, also known as disruptive innovation or uberization. First, there is doubt as to whether an innovation will succeed or not. Many are called, as we all know, but few are chosen. There is a saying that innovation is like throwing pasta at a wall: some of it will stick, but there's no telling which bits. Moreover this is a case of radical uncertainty, not risk, because the proportion of the pasta that will stick to the wall is unknown. In more scientific terms, we cannot determine the probability of the innovation succeeding. Indeed it may not even obey any particular law. Even in a specific sector no one knows whether they need to launch 10, 100 or 1,000 projects to obtain a commercially viable product or service. If it was known, it would not count as disruptive innovation, just run-of-the-mill incremental innovation. For example, in research to develop new medicines the specialists know roughly how many molecules they need to screen to find one that has a positive outcome for mice, and then how many should turn out to be beneficial to and tolerated by humans, after clinical trials. Due to this intrinsic radical uncertainty, a disruptive innovation can only be identified after the fact, stripping the theory of disruptive innovation of any predictive power. Only observation of market upheaval, with its share of downgraded and failed enterprises, moving borders and shifting patterns of competition, can reveal disruptive innovation. When the first iPhones were rolled out, no one imagined that the device and its apps would lead to such a storm of competition and sell over a billion units!

Uncertainty also clouds the economic prospects of disruptive innovations. This is particularly true at times, such as the present day, when innovations come in waves, in the form of widely used technologies like PCs or smartphones, or artificial intelligence, still in its early days. Do they yield greater productivity? Do they bring growth? Do they generate more jobs than they destroy? In the days when innovation was still referred to as technical progress, as in the nineteenth century, there was little doubt about its benefits for society as a whole. The present term, which caught on in the second half of the twentieth century, has a more neutral connotation. Disruption, which is now taking its place, has a negative, possibly catastrophic meaning. This change reflects the fear of massive jobs losses, dubbed Robocalypse Now by a Massachusetts Institute of Technology economist.[7]

If we look at productivity gains, conventionally used as a macroeconomic indicator of innovation, it appears, surprisingly, to be running out of steam. Some economists even suggest that the reason for this is that, contrary to appearances, the current waves of innovation are not as powerful as those of the past.[8] The driverless car, for instance, will never change the world in the way that the invention of the automobile did. Other economists argue that the loss of momentum is an illusion, due to the shortcomings of measuring instruments, such as growth, which underestimate the effects of innovation.[9] Another common observation is that the positive aggregate impact of productivity gains on jobs is diminishing.[10] Does this trend mean that in the future innovation measured by productivity gains will destroy more jobs overall than it generates, contrary to what we have seen over the past forty years? This is indeed quite possible. There is no inflexible macroeconomic rule dictating that productivity gains will never entail the immiseration of labour.

We may, however, be sure of one thing: disruptive innovation will continue to have a far greater effect on competition than its run-of-the-mill, incremental equivalent. Definitely a bombardment, rather than forcing a door.

Notes

1. Tapscott, D. (1997), *Digital Economy: Promise and Peril in the Age of Networked Intelligence*, New York, McGraw-Hill.
2. Dediu, H. (2012), 'Technology Spectator: retail lessons from Apple and Ikea', *The Australian Business Review*, 8 May 2012.
3. Shapiro, C. (2012), Competition and innovation: Did Arrow Hit the Bull's Eye?, in *The Rate and Direction of Inventive Activity Revisited*, Lerner, J. and Stern, S. (eds.), Chicago IL: University of Chicago Press, pp. 361–404.
4. Gilbert, R. (2006), Looking for Mr. Schumpeter: Where Are We in the Competition-Innovation Debate?, in *Innovation Policy and the Economy*,

vol. 6, Jaffe, A., Lerner, J. and Stern, S. (eds.), Boston, MA: MIT Press, pp. 159–215.

5. Barnett, W. (2016), *The Red Queen Among Organizations: How Competitiveness Evolves*, Princeton, NJ: Princeton University Press.
6. Barthes, R. (1970), *L'Empire des Signes*, Paris: Skira.
7. www.nber.org/confer/2017/AIf17/Autor.pdf.
8. Gordon, R. (2016), *The Rise and Fall of American Growth: The US Standard of Living Since the Civil War*, Princeton, NJ: Princeton University Press.
9. Aghion, Ph. et al. (2017), 'Missing growth from creative destruction', Federal Reserve Bank of San Francisco working papers series.
10. www.nber.org/confer/2017/AIf17/Autor.pdf, ibid.

PART IV

Competition and Redistribution

It has of course to be admitted that the manner in which the benefits and burdens are apportioned by the market mechanism would in many instances have to be regarded as very unjust *if* it were the result of a deliberate allocation to particular people.

F. A. Hayek, *Law, Legislation and Liberty*, 1973

NINETEEN

Bidding for Soccer TV Rights

Top clubs are spending astronomical amounts on soccer star trans-fers and pay. The money comes primarily from sales of television broadcasting rights.

At the beginning of 2018, BSkyB and British Telecom agreed to pay English Premier League clubs £1.47 billion a season, for the following years, to broadcast matches. At the auction in 2012, the two companies forked out half this amount. At the end of the 1990s, the same rights were worth eight times less. In 2014, beIN Sports and Canal+ settled on paying €726 million per season, for the period from 2016 to 2020, to France's Fédération de Football Professionnel for Ligue 1 matches, up 25% on previous years and six times more than 15 years ago. In 2015, Altice, owner of telecommunications and cable operator SFR-Numéricable, purchased exclusive rights for broadcasting English Premier League matches in France, at a cost of €100 million a season. In the previous round, Canal+ had paid €63 million for the same rights.

The Well-Known Benefits of Auctions

It is impossible to grasp why broadcasting rights have soared in this way without knowing how the auctions work. How can the owner of a generally unique good, or series of goods, sell it, or them, for the highest possible price? Through an auction in which all the poten-tial buyers can compete. In this way Les Femmes d'Alger, painted by

Pablo Picasso in 1955, sold for $160 million at Christie's in New York, starting from an initial asking price of $100 million. Several interested parties, located all over the world, made bids by phone until the hammer finally came down. This auction showed that the painting's new owner set a price of $160 million on their satisfaction at acquiring Les Femmes d'Alger, whereas the other bidders' was lower.

The head of the FFP Frédéric Thiriez acted as auctioneer for the sale of France's Ligue 1 rights in spring 2014, assisted by the heads of the various clubs. They spent a whole day together, locked up in a room without their mobile phones or any other means of communicating with the outside world. Certified officials passed on incoming bids from broadcasters received on secure phone lines.

They were using a sequential rather than a rising bidding system. Several packages were up for sale, auctioned one after another. The first package was also the most attractive one, comprising rights for broadcasting two matches a week live, including at least one top game. The sixth and last package was the least interesting, covering rights to broadcasts extracts of all the matches but slightly later. Canal+ took the first two packages, paying €540 million a season; beIN Sports took the rest, at a cost of €160 million a season. With these rights in hand, Canal+ reckoned it would earn at least €2.7 billion over the four-year period, in the form of new subscribers to its service, renewed or higher subscription fees. As for beIN it was counting on the other packages bringing in at least €800 million. Clearly it would not make economic sense to buy a right that did not generate revenue over the long term equal or superior to what it cost.

But Is It Reasonable to Buy Rights?

Good economic sense dictates that a company taking part in an auction should not bid more than the sum of the discounted profits derived from the contract in the event of a successful outcome.

However, there are all sorts of reasons why a company might not be entirely reasonable. Its executive officers might, for instance, not hold shares in the venture, so they would not be spending their own money. In a situation of this sort, they might be tempted to take ill-considered risks. Things are not necessarily any better with share-holders at the helm; they may have deep pockets or be crazy about football. Moreover, there is great uncertainty. Exactly how many new subscribers will such and such exclusive rights attract? How will individual subscribers respond to a higher subscription fee? Who will stay and who will go? In response to how high a rise? In some cases, uncertainty leads to the winner's curse: the bidder winning an auction is simply the most optimistic participant, putting too high a value on the good they purchase.[1] This is a well-known feature of auctions of mining and oil-drilling rights. But a company governed by reason should not fall into this trap, for business executives are supposed to recognize situations in which this curse might strike. Being full aware of the economic theory of auctions, they would on the contrary proceed with great caution![2]

If, then, we assume that companies purchasing football broad-casting rights are indeed reasonable, there are two reasons that explain the current inflation in the amounts paid to premier league organizations: broadcasters are counting on increasing revenue from showing matches and the sellers are capturing an increasing share of this bounty through better-organized auctions.

Two Forces Driving Inflation

Let's start by looking at the second reason. For a long time, BSkyB enjoyed an undisputed monopoly of rights to broadcast English Premier League matches. By splitting the rights into several packages and then preventing a single buyer from acquiring all of them, the League succeeded in bringing greater competition into the game, in the form of an Irish broadcaster and BT. In France, the sequential nature of the FFP auction is a masterstroke. After the first package has been allocated only the winner knows which bid was successful and the amount paid; all the others know is that they lost the first round. Competition to win the second package will be more intense than in a simultaneous auction, in which all the participants file their bids for all the packages at the same time.

By intensifying competition for the purchase of their exclusive rights, organizations such as the Premier League can come close to the absolute limit, which would mean pocketing all the profits bidders expect to derive from subscriptions and advertising. The buyers would pay the League all they earn, making no profit whatsoever on the broadcasting rights they purchase. In economic parlance, we would say that the auction dissipated ex ante the ex post gains of buyers. Competition between bidders to win the contract results, for them, in a situation of perfect competition, in other words, zero profit. Meanwhile the seller pockets all the monopoly, or scarcity, rent.

The Growing Appeal of Football, with Profits to Match

Why do television companies expect revenue from broadcasting football matches to increase? First, because football has growing appeal. Premier League matches draw increasingly large audiences. Their lead over other broadcasts, such as films or big variety shows, is opening up. Furthermore, viewers watching football matches live are particularly valuable. They are immune to the temptation to replay programmes and skip adverts, so the corresponding revenue is lost. Other things being equal, with more paying subscribers and more pairs of eyes viewing the adverts, broadcasters can afford to pay more for exclusive rights. From this point of view, the entry of telephone operators and Internet service providers, such as BT or Altice, changes the picture. They can spread the cost of football rights bought to boost the appeal of their multiplay bundles over a much larger number of subscribers.

Second, because a larger share of the contents of viewers' pockets is hoovered up. Competition to buy exclusive rights has encouraged broadcasters to innovate and programme quality has improved. Matches are sandwiched between pre and post-match shows featuring news and analysis, taking cameras into dressing rooms, interviewing soccer stars and such. In addition, multiplex offers and solutions for only watching specific games have flourished. So broadcasters are closing in on the maximum amount that consumers are prepared to pay. To watch all English Premier League games (154 per season), sports fans must fork out about £500 a year.

Lastly, where do the proceeds of auctions go? The lion's share goes to the clubs, which in turn spend most of it on buying and paying players. Competition between premier league clubs in Europe to attract soccer talent, particularly strikers, has become extreme.

To sum up, the more football leagues earn from exclusive rights, thanks in particular to feverish competition between buyers, the more they empty fans' pockets and the more agents, trainers and players earn ... which by extension tops up the bank accounts of dealers selling Ferraris, Aston Martins, Maseratis and other flash, fast cars.

Notes

1. https://en.wikipedia.org/wiki/Winner's curse.
2. Klemperer, P. (2004), *Auctions: Theory and Practice*, Princeton, NJ: Princeton University Press.

TWENTY

For and Against Fixed Retail Book Prices

What would happen in France if the 1981 law instituting a fixed retail price for books was repealed? Would it sound the death-knell for independent bookshops? Might it bring the average price of books down? Would general-interest, self-help books sell better, to the detriment of niche novels?

Given the broad consensus in favour of fixed prices among French voters, it is a largely theoretical question for the time being. Indeed this legal constraint has recently been extended to e-books. But it does have the merit of casting some light on the economic effects of such measures, some of which are surprising as you will see. Moreover, the issue is extremely controversial in other countries. In a referendum in 2012, the Swiss voted against re-instating the fixed book-price agreement, whereas some people in the United Kingdom, which shelved the system 20 years ago, are calling for its return.[1]

Before analysing in greater detail the effects of fixed book prices, let's look at the basic principle and its aims.[2] This system empowers publishers to set the retail price of books, whether they are sold by bookshops or supermarkets. More exactly, for each of its books the publisher sets a price that is marked near the bottom of the back cover; the retailer cannot reduce this price by more than 5%. In other words, the publisher, which also decides the wholesale price of its products, controls retail mark-up and drastically limits any scope for discounts and special offers.

With this measure the legislator aims to achieve several effects, the first of which is to guarantee equal treatment. Consumers pay the same price, regardless of whether they live in a city or the country-side, whether they shop in a hypermarket, the local newsagent's, at one of the Fnac retail outlets or a traditional bookseller's. Second, it seeks to keep alive a network of independent retailers stocking a wide range of works. Third, it strives to secure diversity of produc-tion, including books for special-interest groups. So much for the good intentions; what of the facts?

The End of a Collective Agreement in Britain

The British example is instructive, a real-life experiment for obser-ving the effects of such a measure, with thirty years of free-floating prices following almost a century of fixed prices. So we can easily compare the differences between the two periods.

On the question of equal treatment, the result is beyond doubt, even if the British system was far from watertight under the old arrangement. Unlike France, fixed book prices were instituted by the Net Book Agreement.[3] The publishers collectively set a retail price for booksellers; in the event of non-compliance the latter ran the risk of supplies being stopped. The effectiveness of this threat began to wear a bit thin in the late 1980s. With the growing volume of books sold by big retailers and chain stores, punishing special offers on certain books by halting deliveries meant losing an outlet, tantamount for the publishers to shooting themselves in the foot. So in practice shoppers could find different prices here and there.

However, ending the NBA brought about disparities of an alto-gether different magnitude. One example is quite sufficient: had you set out, in March 2003, to buy a paperback copy of *Bad Boy Jack* by Josephine Cox, you would have paid £6.99 at Sainsbury's, £5.43 at Waterstones, £4.99 at WHSmith and £3.51 at Tesco.[4]

Impact on Retail Network

The end of the NBA also had a significant impact on distribution channels. In 1995, some 2,000 independent bookshops accounted for 28% of total sales. Their number has been halved since then, with sales plummeting to less than 5%.[5] Consumer purchases have shifted to chain stores, supermarkets and, of course, the Internet, for both conventional and e-books. Independent booksellers have suffered from the loss of revenue and mark-up from sales of bestsellers, depriving them of the means to cover the cost of providing advice and sustaining stock levels. In addition, they have little bargaining power when dealing with publishers. It should be noted that, apart from supermarkets, the distribution channels which have supplanted traditional booksellers represent, at the very least, an equivalent investment. Between 1993 and 1999, WHSmith and Waterstones tripled the average size of their shops,[6] which suggests that the number of books on the shelves must have increased too. However, the increase is probably not proportional, because sofas, coffee tables and other amenities take up quite a lot of room.

On the other hand, the diversity of production does not seem to have changed. Growth in the number of new titles being published has continued at much the same rate as before, with 65,000 new titles in 1990, 100,000 in 1996 and 130,000 in 2003.[7] That figure has now reached 200,000.

However, it would be unreasonable to attribute all these changes to the end of fixed retail prices! This is a classic problem with descriptive statistics and the observation of correlations. For instance, the decline of independent bookshops and the increasing clout of other distribution channels are partly due to other causes, in particular the rising price of retail property in town centres. Similarly sustained growth of the number of new titles does not in itself prove that ending fixed prices had no effect. It may simply be concealed by other factors.

In other words, maintaining the fixed-price system might have generated even higher growth. To demonstrate relations of cause and effect specific to the end of fixed prices would require detailed econometric research, which, to the best of my knowledge, has been not been carried out for books in the United Kingdom. The only consequence that can be attributed with any certainty to liberalization is the disparity of prices, for otherwise the special offers would not be possible. As for the disappearance of independent bookshops, all that can said – particularly as the same trend has been observed and studied elsewhere – is that ending fixed prices was one of the causes, without being able to determine its relative significance.[8]

Once Unchained, Prices Go Up and Down

How much effect does the price have? Has the 1981 law in France, and comparable measures in other countries, driven book prices up? One's intuition would suggest that it has. Such measures eliminate scope for competition on prices between retailers and prevent *de facto* substantial discounts. In practice things are a little more complicated.

Returning to the British case, according to a study by Professor Stephen Davies, at University of East Anglia, the price of books fell after the NBA was scrapped.[9] However Frank Fishwick, an economist at Cranfield University, observed an increase. Actually both authors are right. The latter looked at changes in the average price of books, whereas the former focussed on the average price of books weighted by the quantities sold. In the first case, the price of Harry Potter and the Philosopher's Stone counts as one, much as any other published book, whereas in the second case it counts as several million. Furthermore, whereas some titles, such as J. K. Rowling's novels, sold at knockdown prices, the price of others increased. So liberalization actually had two effects in this respect: the price of bestsellers dropped, the price of books for special-interest groups rose.

It is impossible to foresee the results of these two effects, because we do not know what the new equilibrium price is. It isn't even possible to estimate them properly because we do not know the price elasticity of demand either. All we do know is that the people who read books lauded by the critics but printed in small quantities also read a great deal, frequent city-centre bookshops and are relatively insensitive to price variations, often because they are fairly well-heeled. In contrast, a larger share of the population is much more sensitive to price differences, so discounts increase the volume of sales. So it is impossible to say whether repealing existing French legislation on the retail price of books would lead to an increase or decrease in the average price of books weighted by quantity. We might however venture to suggest that the average price, unweighted by the volume of sales, would increase, simply because there are far fewer bestsellers than other, less popular works.

Bear in mind that by preventing both discounts and surcharges the current rules in France have a regressive effect well-known to economists specializing in cultural goods: households in the lowest income groups pay a higher price for books, whereas those in the highest income brackets pay a lower price.[10]

Stated more bluntly, the fixed price entails a subsidy for people who read a lot, living in comfort, with a taste for literature and scientific or historical works, the subsidy being funded by people who read less or earn less and have little interest in fiction and learned treatises.

Notes

1. 'Prix unique du livre: tous les yeux fixés sur la Comco', Fédération Romande des Consommateurs, 12 March 2012.
2. www.culture.gouv.fr/culture/dll/prix-livre/prix-1.htm.
3. Net Book Agreement, Wikipedia.
4. Davies, S. et al. (2004), 'The benefits from competition: some illustrative UK cases', Centre for Economics Policy, University of East Anglia, Department of Trade and Industry Economics Paper 9.

5. *Global Fixed Book Price Report* (2014), International Publishers Association.
6. Davies et al., 'The benefits from competition', ibid.
7. Fishwick, F. (2008), 'Book retailing in the UK since the abandonment of fixed prices', Washington, DC: Institute for Local Self-Reliance.
8. Perona, M. and Pouyet, J. (2010), *Le Prix Unique du Livre à l'Heure du Numérique*, Paris: Les Editions de la Rue d'Ulm.
9. Davies,et al. 'The benefits from competition', ibid.
10. Benhamou, F. (2011), *L'Economie de la Culture*, Paris: Editions La Découverte.

TWENTY ONE

Gyms Running on Empty

The business model of many gyms is based on absentee members. They sign up for a year, often in early January, drop in a few times over the first few months, then give up. Members of this sort are really useful, underpinning the business model of mid-range fitness centres. However, with the appearance of low-cost gyms, this model is under threat.

Club Goods

Sports centres are club goods. This apparent tautology conceals a service shared exclusively by several people, for example a private swimming pool or tennis court belonging to a block of flats. The particular feature of this sort of good is that the satisfaction an individual derives from it depends on the other users. On the one hand, the larger the number of members, the less each one will need to contribute to the fixed costs related to the initial outlay and upkeep. But on the other hand, the more members there are, the greater the pressure of demand on the good will be.

Accepting a new member means the annual fee for access to the pool and tennis court can be reduced, but swimmers may bump into one another in the water and players won't always be able to practise at their favourite time. So a sports centre is a club good, in the economic sense of the term: increasing the number of members will enable the membership fee to be reduced, but it will make for longer queues for the exercise machines and showers.

A classic, but quite 'beefy' exercise involves calculating the optimal capacity for a given number of members (for example, the appropriate size of a swimming pool for fifty residents), and the optimal number of members for a given capacity (ideal number for an 8-by-4-metre pool) in order to obtain the optimal capacity for the optimal number. All this should be done by specifying a cost function that takes into account economies of scale and a profit function allowing for the fact that after a while congestion matters more than good company. Accepting a new member increases scope for making new friends, but this gain pales before the congestion the newcomer may cause. James Buchanan, winner of the Nobel prize for economics in 1986, was the first to wrestle with this theoretical exercise.

One-Year Subscriptions Are Key

Meanwhile, the owners of gyms and fitness centres have understood the advantages of demanding a one-year commitment from members, many of whom rarely use the facility, if at all. This category reduces the annual fee paid by all members without creating any congestion. In the United States, almost half the new members enrolling at the beginning of January, when applications peak, no longer use the facility a few months later. Only one in five new members will still be coming back the following September. On average, new members use the sports centre four times in the 12 months following enrolment. According to a study of 1,500 new members of Montreal gyms by Canadian researchers, attendance rates at fitness centres drop by half after four months.[1]

Yet the newcomers enrol of their own free will and do not object to committing themselves to a year's membership, contrary to what they would do for a mobile phone or subscription-television service. So why are they prepared to pay not to go to the gym? In an article

164 • Gyms Running on Empty

published by the American Economic Review in 2006, two econo-mists sought to answer this question.[2] They calculated that consumers were losing about $600. This is what a member choosing a one-year plan pays over and above what they would spend if they chose a pay-per-visit option covering 10 admissions. The difference may be explained by optimism or naivety. When they sign up, people tend to overestimate the number of times they will use the facility.

Intention and Real Use

In the Canadian study cited above, when new members enrolled, they stated the number of times they planned to visit the gym. Their actual attendance, observed subsequently, was half the amount. We tend to believe in the lasting effect of our New Year resolutions to lose weight or simply keep fit. In the present case, they may also have been counting on an incentive effect: 'I've paid so I must get a return on my outlay.' Whatever the explanation, it didn't work out.

Absentee members enable sports clubs to charge lower fees . . . or make a handsome profit. It all depends on how intense competition is. If there are no other gym clubs in the vicinity, the owner can pocket most of the surplus derived from absentees. Competition in this sort of game is local, with customers choosing a gym close to their workplace or home. But in addition to spatial competition, allowance must be made for the quality of services.

Segmentation

The fitness market breaks down into three segments. Premium clubs charge membership fees in excess of €100 a month. Prospective members may need to be sponsored by someone already belonging to the club and pay a joining fee. With stylish, sometimes garish, interior decorations, scope for one-to-one coaching, space to relax and a big swimming pool, such gyms are pretty luxurious. The Ritz

Health Club, in Paris, is open to athletes not staying at the hotel (€3,900 a year or €180 a day, whichever you prefer).

Mid-range centres, charging between €50 and €100 a month, represent the soft underbelly of the market. Customers are given a clean towel on arrival, can perspire in a sauna or hammam, and enjoy a drink at the bar, but everything is finely calculated. This market segment is now subject to keen competition from budget gyms.

Low-cost gyms first appeared in the USA. There is plenty of space and leases have been cheap since the financial crash. They then spread to the United Kingdom and are now catching on in Europe, driving a 10% rise in club membership. Regardless of whether they are called Xercise4Less, Budget Gym or Fitness4Less, the message is the same. The business model too: low monthly fee, open 24/7, minimal services. No sauna or hammam here (costly, little-used extras), no group lessons (or only on a video), no staff to help with the machines (except from 18.00 to 22.00), no (expensive) full-length mirrors, no courtesy towel (remember to bring your own), and a charge for a shower (€0.50 at Neoness).

On the other, hand prices are unbeatable. Packages at $10, £10 or €10 are now on offer in all major cities, generally on the out-skirts, where rents are lowest. Budget gyms require no contractual commitment. Their business model does not depend on absentee members, rather on cutting costs and trimming prices. They are attracting new adepts but also the price-sensitive customers of mid-range gyms.

Tightening Up the Soft Underbelly

Low-cost gyms have about 5,000 members on average, compared to 1,900 for the market as a whole.[3] They are also better at keeping their customers. The latter no longer make naïve or optimistic long-term commitments, nor are they disappointed by their own patchy attendance, which used to mean they wouldn't renew their subscription at the end of the year.

Sandwiched between premium and low-cost clubs, the owners of mid-range gyms are in trouble. In 2014, almost 300 clubs in this segment in Canada closed. In the meantime, twice that number of low-cost operations started trading.

To avoid being wiped out, the solution for mid-priced clubs is to offer attractively priced luxury services or drastically reduce costs, prices and the length of contracts. In time this will bring changes to their members. Absentees with little real inclination to pump iron or ride an elliptical bike will stop subsidizing their more athletic counterparts with six-pack abs or the heart of a Zumba dancer.

Notes

1. Garon, J-D., Masse, A. and Michaud, P-C. (2014), 'Health club attendance, expectations and self-control', CESifo working paper 4926.
2. Vigna, S. and Malmendier, U. (2006), 'Paying Not to Go to the Gym', *American Economic Review*, 96(3): 694–719.
3. 'It works out cheaper. Cut-price gyms are seizing a growing share of a stagnant market', *The Economist*, 1 November 2014.

TWENTY TWO

Phantom Economics at the Opera

Much as other cultural bodies, opera houses are non-profit-making organizations. They are subsidized by national and local government, and supported by private patrons. For example, the French state pays Opéra National de Paris €130 for each seat it sells, on top of about €10 m in annual earnings from well-meaning sponsors, companies and private individuals. Opera houses are nevertheless exposed to competition and, though under no obligation to make a profit, they must balance their books, an increasingly acrobatic exercise.

An Opera House in Every City?

A few years ago New York City Opera went bankrupt.[1] Seventy years earlier it had opened with Tosca, Giacomo Puccini's classic tragedy. It wound up proceedings with Anna Nicole, based on the life of a rags-to-riches Playboy playmate. She married an octogenarian, but he died soon afterwards. Ten years passed, Nicole put on weight, lost her son, became deranged and died. This modern saga, loved by the audience but lambasted by critics, was not enough to revive the flagging finances of the City Opera. Nor was it staged by its rather up-market rival, the Metropolitan Opera.

New York City, with its two rival establishments (the City Opera re-opened in 2016), and London, with the Royal Opera House at Covent Garden and Saddlers Wells, home to the equally illustrious but slightly shaky English National Opera, are exceptions.[2] As is Berlin, which has boasted three opera houses since Reunification. But here all three venues are now managed by a single foundation, a move that has so far preserved them all. It also means that the programme is co-ordinated. The same opera being staged on the same day at all three locations – as once happened for the Mozart's Magic Flute – was an unfortunate coincidence never to recur.

Otherwise, one opera house is the rule, even for big cities. But this apparent monopoly does not altogether eliminate competition.

Local Monopoly, Global Competition

Opera houses must compete to attract talent: eminent conductors in residence and experienced chief executives, famous directors and guest performers all contribute to boosting international prestige. But without wishing to offend these remarkable people, to an economist they are scarcely any different from the most sought after soccer players. Top talents are rare, witness the fees opera houses are prepared to pay. Bear in mind that the reproduction of music by the gramophone and its successors has accentuated the star system among opera singers, opening up the gap between their earnings. Alfred Marshall, an eminent British economist, cited the example of an opera singer, who, despite her considerable fame, did not command an audience much larger than other sopranos. The amount she could hope to earn was limited by the number and size of opera houses. She simply filled halls a little more effectively and performed more often in the top venues than her fellows. So despite her fame, her market share was much the same as her rivals. The invention of recording obviously changed the rules of the game. The audience of superstars, such as the late Pavarotti, amounts to hundreds of millions of people, measured by the number of records they sell.[3] Such mega-fame, fuelled by recordings, necessarily has an impact on the fees singers can demand from opera houses. This is a good example of how enlarging a market can amplify disparities in commercial success.[4]

However, the fees of leading singers are still very modest compared to what football stars earn. Above all, unlike the clubs, opera houses don't stage nail-biting matches between their respective teams!

Such competition plays out in terms of notoriety. Competition between states and cities for the best opera house goes back to the days of kingdoms and courts. Germany is the most striking instance. In the years before 1800, kings, princes and dukes in search of grandeur built more than thirty opera houses on the ruins of a fragmented empire. Nor was this enthusiasm the exclusive preserve of the rich and powerful. An econometrically solid study has shown that urban prosperity was not behind the decision to build baroque theatres.[5]

Rewarding Prestige

However cities did become richer if they took this course. Its prestige enhanced, it could attract better-educated, more enterprising people, fuelling stronger growth. These days it seems unlikely that such expectations are behind contemporary projects such as Opéra Bastille, in Paris, or the Dubai Opera, less still the effect they produce. No, competition for prestige alone is still a powerful impetus.

Furthermore, a monopoly exists in relation to a market. It may vanish if the borders of the market expand outwards, the organization no longer holding a 100% market share. Accordingly Opéra de Paris, which runs the original Palais Garner opera house and recent Bastille addition, enjoys a monopoly of opera staged in the French capital (I trust the directors of much smaller venues such as Théâtre des Champs Elysées or Bouffes du Nord will forgive me for overlooking them).

But might it not be more to the point to consider a broader market including symphonic music, for instance: the same people enjoy opera and classical music; and they can only consume one or the other at any given time.

The Curse of Rising Costs

If we accept that they are substitutable – in other words, an increase in the price of one significantly increases consumption of the other – then the market should be extended. In Helsinki, a 10% increase in the price of other artistic events prompts an equivalent rise in demand for seats at the Finnish National Opera.[6]

Opera and concerts, indeed all live entertainment (performed on stage by flesh-and-blood artists), share another economic characteristic: the curse of rising costs. William Baumol, a polymath economist and genius, theorized and demonstrated this disease.[7] The key feature is not that live actors, singers or musicians are involved; they are no different in this respect from other agents producing goods or services. The key economic property is that the work of the performer is not a means of production for manufacturing something, but the product itself. As a result, not much can be done to increase productivity. Four musicians are still needed to play one of Beethoven's opus eighteen-string quartets, just as when they were first performed in 1801, and it would be outrageous to attempt to perform such a work in less than 20 minutes.[8] However, per capita productivity has substantially increased in other sectors, as have wages. Obviously, there is no question of trying to keep the earnings of live entertainers at the same level as when the works were first published. The members of the chorus who appear as slaves in Verdi's Nabucco, prisoners of the Babylonians, but not of an opera house in Paris or Milan. They too should earn a fair wage.

Short of replacing performing artists with holograms, the cost of operas, concerts or ballets will inevitably outstrip that of other goods and services, and the average income of households. Over a period of a little more than a century, the cost per concert of the New York Philharmonic orchestra has increased by 2.5% a year, compared with just 1% for the consumer price index in the United States. Looking at a shorter period, from 1951 to 1964, the average cost per show at the Metropolitan has risen by 4% a year, as against only 0.3% for the consumer price index.[9]

Revenue, Subsidy and Sponsorship

To avoid running at a loss, which if it becomes endemic will lead to closure, opera houses have no option but to steadily increase revenue. For a long time in Europe, the simplest solution was to demand greater public subsidies. But that is no longer an option, now the state has budget difficulties of its own. Indeed public support has been known to drop: in 2005–2013, government subsidies to Opéra National de Paris fell by 10%, allowing for inflation.[10] Growing resentment of what many see as an elite pastime has also hampered public support. The state awards the Paris Opera about €100 m a year, equivalent to roughly €130 for every seat it sells.[11] It is hard to imagine government forking out any more in the foreseeable future.

Hence, the growing appetite for private sponsorship. The heads of opera houses in France, Germany and Italy must now raise funds from companies and rich donors, just like their US counterparts. The latter have longstanding experience in this field, their establishments having long depended largely on the private sector for funding. Opéra National de Paris can now count on the solid and effective support of a society of benefactors, Association pour le Rayonnement de l'Opéra de Paris, which raised some €13 m in 2016.[12]

But the price of seats is rising too, up by an average of 30% in the French capital in only eight years (2005–2013).[13] However, this figure hides considerable disparity: to maximize ticket office revenue, opera houses use price discrimination. According to a basic economic principle, companies enjoying a monopoly should apply different prices to derive the greatest value from consumers. Obviously the latter's willingness to pay depends on their interest in a particular good or service, and their budget constraints.

Price Discrimination

In a theatre or opera house, price discrimination is made easier by the position of seats in relation to the stage. Their distance and view vary, so categories of seat can be sold at different prices despite the fact that their cost to the venue is exactly the same. So discrimination between opera buffs works as follows: those with the greatest willingness to pay will opt for the most expensive seats commanding the best view, whereas those least willing to pay will settle for the worst seats. At Palais Garnier in Paris there are currently seven categories of seat. You should allow €200 for the top bracket, in the stalls or grand tier, whereas the most affordable seats are only €10, seats in the boxes on the side of the auditorium commanding only a very limited view of the stage. It may seem odd that such seats should exist at all, but there was a time in Italian-style theatres, such as Garnier, when it was more important to be seen at the opera by other spectators than to see the show itself.

There is no reason to take offence at such discrimination, for it allows for a more diverse audience than would be possible if everyone paid the same for their seat. Those paying the highest price certainly get the best view, but they contribute much more to the fixed cost of the opera, in some sense subsidizing those who pay the least. Nor should we be shocked to learn that Opéra National de Paris has split the top category, putting the very best seats in a separate group called Optima, with an even higher price. What is less apparent, is that the opera house has reshuffled other seats, upgrading them to the top-but-one category.[14] So at Opéra Bastille there are now more 'top' seats than before, yet none of them have moved an inch since the place was built!

In Search of Blockbusters

Adapting the repertoire is the ultimate expedient for boosting revenue and dodging the curse of rising costs. staging more sure-fire successes, fewer modern works and more first performances, in particular. Readers who like rankings, may look at Operabase, which reports that the most popular composers are Verdi (Traviata, Rigoletto), Mozart (Magic Flute, Figaro, Don Juan) and Puccini (Bohème, Tosca, Madame Butterfly).[15]

This trio penned a third of all the works staged worldwide during the last five seasons. Wagner is in fifth place, behind Rossini. Bizet does not rate a mention, Carmen being his only favourite. The first living composer in the ranking is Philip Glass, in 41st place.

Those who prefer a more econometric approach will enjoy a study of the Finnish National Opera, which shows that demand for first nights is much greater than for revivals, for Finnish works rather than the rest of the classical repertoire, and for the Ring cycle rather than other classics.[16] Recruiting a big star has much greater effect at a first night than at a revival. Demand is higher in November than any other month; Fridays and Saturdays draw much bigger audiences than any other day of the week.

Staging Less Costly Works

However, what they win on the swings they may lose on the roundabouts. Some blockbusters cost more than others. First nights are necessarily more expensive than revivals. The leading roles in Verdi's Aida need the support of a dazzling cast, so despite its enormous popularity it is rarely staged. Less often, for instance than Rigoletto or Die Fledermaus by Johann Strauss.

Molière reputedly asserted that 'Of all the noises known to man, opera is the most expensive.' It takes outstanding management gifts to achieve its economic harmony. The heads of opera houses must maintain artistic standards, keep an eye on competition from other venues and forms of live entertainment, juggle with three sources of funding, sell seats at just the right price, strike a balance between premières and revivals, between ancient and modern, not to mention the need to appeal to various audiences, bring in newcomers, stage ballets at regular intervals, and cope with capricious prima donnas or staff, with their firmly established rights.

Although they are running non-profit organizations with a local monopoly, the management of opera houses need to be every bit as clever as the CEOs of profit-making corporations.

Notes

1. 'Final curtains', *The Economist*, 3 October 2013.
2. Maddocks, F. (2016), 'ENO in crisis: who can keep the magic alive?', *The Guardian*.
3. www.scena.org/columns/lebrecht/070321-NL-classic.html.
4. Rosen, S. (1981), 'The economics of superstars', *The American Economic Review*, 71(5): 845–858.
5. Falck, O., Fritsch, M. and Heblich, S. (2011), 'The phantom of the opera: cultural amenities, human capital, and regional economic growth', *Labour Economics*, 18(6): 755–766.
6. Laamanen, J-P. (2013), 'Estimating demand for opera using sales system data: the case of Finnish National Opera', *Journal of Cultural Economics*, 37(4): 417–432
7. Baumol, W. and Bowen, W. (1966), *Performing Arts: The Economic Dilemma, a Study of Problems, Common to Theater, Opera, Music and Dance*, Cambridge, MA: The Twentieth Century Fund.
8. Heilbrun, J. (2003), Baumol's Cost Disease, in *A Handbook of Cultural Economics*, Cheltenham, UK: Edward Elgar Publishing.
9. Baumol and Bowen. *Performing Arts*.
10. www.ccomptes.fr/fr/publications/lopera-national-de-paris

11. Ibid.
12. www.arop-opera.com/home
13. www.ccomptes.fr/fr/publications/lopera-national-de-paris, ibid.
14. www.ccomptes.fr/fr/publications/lopera-national-de-paris, ibid.
15. http://operabase.com/top.cgi
16. Laamanen, 'Estimating demand for opera using sales system data', ibid.

TWENTY THREE

Uber, or Forget About Taxis and Drivers for a While

Uber is the bête noire of cab companies, but over a million drivers worldwide are using its platform. Let's forget about the former for a moment and disregard their losses and the question of whether the competition facing this regulated trade is fair, or not. Let's also set aside the question of whether Uber drivers used to be jobless and now have an occupation or are just more exploited gig-economy workers. Let's look, instead, at the benefits for consumers and at competition in ride-hailing services.

Various Issues Depending on the National Context

Uber's sudden entry into the world of urban transport sparked, and still sparks, much debate. The biggest controversies centre on allegations that the regulatory framework governing hire cabs is ill suited to the Uber business model, on possible ways of updating that framework, on loss of revenue by cab-drivers and the price of their licences, but also on the number of jobs created by Uber's ride-hailing service, their value to society (casual labour or genuine jobs, rock-bottom or decent wages) and their contractual details (disguised employees or self-employed contractors). In other words, the key controversy relates to rivalry between Uber and conventional cabs, its causes and effects.

Such debate is legitimate and deserves consideration. But any insights will depend on local or national conditions. The regulatory framework governing cabs, labour law and the level of unemployment vary from one big city or country to another. For the time being, the analysis that has been published has focused on only a small number of geographically delimited markets.

Take for example the background and employment record of Uber drivers in France and the United States. In France, a quarter of them were previously unemployed half of them spend more than 30 hours a week at the wheel; and for three-quarters, a large share of their income is dependent on work for Uber.[1] In the USA, under 10% of Uber drivers were previously out of work and for the vast majority it is a part-time job, supplementing their existing earnings.[2]

In France, Uber drivers make up a larger share of the local workforce in areas of high unemployment and low median wages.[3] In the USA, on the contrary, there is little distinction between Uber drivers and the rest of the working population of big cities.

Put more simply, Uber is an opportunity for those in the USA with insufficient earnings, and in France for those earning nothing. This difference relates to a series specific economic circumstances, but also to the fact that the French authorities would not allow Uber Pop, which would have facilitated part-time work, as in the United States.

The Advantage for the Consumer

So let's concentrate on consumers. The first time you used a ride-hailing service such as Uber you may have had the impression you had entered a different world: a driver who opens the car door for you; who is extremely friendly, asks if you want to listen to the radio and if so which station; who offers you sweets and mineral water. You may also have avoided the smell of dog on the back seat, a general lack of cleanliness, drivers moaning endlessly about the traffic, their refusal to take credit cards and so on.

You may also have noticed that, under pressure from ride-hailing services, the quality of service in Paris cabs has substantially improved. The same is the case in Chicago, where the number of complaints by passengers has dropped since Uber started trading, in particular complaints about rude behaviour, faulty heating and talking on the phone while driving.[4]

Another benefit for consumers delivered by Uber and a few other organizations such as Heetch, is that they offer a service that is no longer restricted to city centres, with better after-hours availability too. A study carried out in New York City showed that there were twice as many Uber rides outside Manhattan as with conventional Yellow Cabs.[5] In France, trips with a ride-hailing service are 50% longer than those made with regular cabs between midnight and the early morning.[6] Millions of consumers, who never used to travel by taxi, now book rides with their smartphone.

Price and Value

If we look at price now, comparison is more complicated. Consumers generally stand to gain, in so far as they may now opt for low-cost services. Car-sharing with Uber Pool or hiring a part-time driver through Uber Pop, for example, makes for much cheaper trips than with a conventional cab. In the USA, where these services are widely available, Uber is cheaper in the vast majority of cities.[7] In Paris, with no access to Uber Pop, the cost of rides booked through (the incumbent) G7 or Uber X is comparable.[8]

To quantify the benefit for consumers, economists calculate the difference between how much they pay and how much they would be ready to pay. For instance, if it's raining, you will pay €10 for a ride, whereas you were actually ready to pay €18 to avoid being drenched. The gain of €8 is your surplus.

A group of US economists estimated the surplus for Uber users transported in 2015 in the USA to be close to $7 billion.[9] Translated into figures that are maybe more meaningful, the average Uber user pockets a $1.57 surplus for every $1 they spend.

Pricing Innovation

This estimate was not obtained by questioning users, but thanks to a form of dynamic pricing known as surge pricing. Rides may be more expensive when everyone comes out of the cinema, if it's raining or at lunchtime on Sundays when drivers would rather stay at home with their families. A multiplier applied to the base rate, typically 1.8x or 2.5x, appears on the display and the consumer clicks to accept the ride or rejects the offer.

This data was used to plot the demand curve and calculate consumer surplus. It tells us, for instance, that 64% of the time consumers accept the price of the ride without a multiplier, but only 39% of the time with a 2x multiplier.

However, scope for making such calculations is not the prime merit of a pricing system that adapts almost instantaneously to the prevailing supply and demand. Above all, it manages scarcity.

First, attracted by the likelihood of more highly paid rides, drivers will head for areas where they are in the greatest demand, adapting their schedule to be there at times of peak demand. And it really works.[10] Observation has shown that the number of Uber rides in New York City rises by 25% when it rains.[11] With a flat pricing system, the number of available vehicles would have been the same and customers would have to have waited a long time or not found a ride at all.

Second, the consumers catching a ride will be those who value the service most highly. With flat pricing, the first-come-first-served rule would be used to manage scarcity. The available vehicles would have been taken regardless of how much more, or less, consumers were ready to pay. For example, the third in line at the taxi rank would have waited their turn, despite being ready to pay more than the people at the front of the queue.

What Is Behind the Price of a Ride?

Now you may be thinking that it's fine if there are more Uber vehicles when it rains but it's not fair for people with more money to be served first. Indeed you may be a hard line advocate of absolute equality. But bear in mind that with an invariable flat rate drivers actually earn less. Nor would they be properly rewarded for the additional effort of staying at the wheel when it rains, despite the congestion, or at lunchtime on Sundays.

The higher price of the ride above all benefits the drivers, with Uber only taking a 20% cut. Bear in mind too that consumers as a whole benefit: with more vehicles available, the gain from the additional riders transported generally exceeds the loss incurred by those who must find a cheaper form of transport, the Uber price being too high.

However, you may not be fully convinced by these arguments, all the more so if you've heard that Uber increased its prices fourfold during the Sydney siege in 2014.[12]

It took Uber several hours to respond and take control of its algorithm, offering free rides and shouldering the burden of paying the higher rate to its drivers. On the other hand, during the terror attacks in central Paris in November 2015 the drivers of conventional cabs, Uber and other ride-hailing vehicles displayed considerable bravery and generosity assisting the injured and transporting hundreds of people free of charge. Conversely, there is no denying that on New Year's Eve Uber prices may be multiplied by five in New York and Paris. [13,14]

What seems to shock most people about the multiplier used by Uber and its rivals, such as Lyft, is a sense of it being unfair. For one thing, some drivers take advantage of the situation for no good reason. Vehicles may just happen to be in a zone where demand suddenly outstrips supply, triggering a price multiplier. These drivers did not deliberately enter the neighbourhood, yet they benefit from the higher rate. It is, so to speak, a godsend!

Asymmetrical Sharing

But above all, our behaviour is not consistent with what is known as economic rationality. The refusal to trade in the case of asymmetric sharing of a loss or gain is a well-known result in experimental economics. It is based on the following experiment: one player, the proposer, receives a sum of money and must offer to share it, as seems fit, with a second player, the responder; the latter may accept or reject the offer; but if they reject the offer all the money is lost for both players.[15] In most cases, if the share-out leaves less than 30% of the total to the responder, they refuse the offer, preferring to gain nothing rather than pocket the money; they feel it is more important to show the proposer that their approach to sharing is unfair. The responder thus punishes the proposer, because they gain nothing either.

A classic method deployed by vendors to reduce the number of buyers rejecting spot price increases, thus limiting the negative impact on their image, entails wholly or partly exonerating loyal customers. As far as I know, Uber has not resorted to this practice, but it is possible that other ride-hailing platforms have done or are preparing to do so. We should not forget that Uber faces other competitors, apart from conventional cabs.

A Global, yet Very Local Market

Uber enjoys a substantial lead over its rivals on account of its geographical coverage. Headquartered in San Francisco, California, the company is now operating in 72 countries and 425 cities. But it does not dominate the market in all cases. It is certainly ahead of Lyft and Curb in almost all US cities, much as in France it leads Chauffeur Privé and LeCab. On the other hand, it is trailing far behind Yandex in Russia, Gojek in Indonesia, Ola in India, and Didi Chuxing in China.[16] These are all local firms. Nor is this surprising because the market for cab rides is by definition local.[17] Furthermore, it may be a decisive asset to understand local conditions, particularly the regulatory framework and politics.

Deploying a global strategy of this sort obviously costs Uber dear. Quickly achieving high market share is essential in this business. Otherwise drivers, carrying too few riders, will not earn enough and customers will wait too long.

Conversely, the higher the number of riders, the lower the rate per kilometre can fall, because drivers are almost always carrying one or more passengers. But to win market share off competitors, vendors must offer attractive prices and discounts. In China, Uber lost $2 billion in two years obstinately disputing Didi's supremacy. In the end, it threw in the sponge, sold its Chinese subsidiary and paid an undisclosed amount for an 18% share in Didi.

Such alliances are common practice for Uber and its counterparts. Lyft, for instance, has joined forces with Ola in India and with Grab in southeast Asia. Bear in mind too that business pacts or joint investments are not restricted to ride-hailing services in their present state.

Uber is a partner with Volvo and Nissan, Lyft is associated with General Motors, Daimler owns MyTaxi. The Internet giants are well represented too. Apple has invested $1 billion in Didi, which also counts Tencent and Alibaba among its shareholders. Google was one of the first to invest in Uber and until recently David Drummond, senior vice president of corporate development at Alphabet, was on its board.[18]

Competition in the Future ... with No Drivers

All these players are busy preparing for future competition, with the likelihood that driverless vehicles will replace private cars. What is the point in owning a car if the streets and avenues are served by smart, four-wheeled vehicles that can be hailed electronically?

What is more, mobility of this sort would represent a smaller annual outlay than car ownership.

The target market does not cover just a few per cent of urban car journeys but virtually all of them. It's the next big thing, which explains why Uber's market value is nearly $50 billion, an amount similar to General Motors, the leading US automobile manufacturer.

We cannot be sure though that Uber will come out on top of this driverless mode of personal transport. The company currently operates without owning much in the way of material assets, most of the vehicles belonging to their drivers. In the future, it will have to operate its own vehicles in a low-margin industry similar to low-cost airlines.[19] But thanks to its capacity for innovation, Uber stands a chance of successfully negotiating this major transformation. But of course it too may be uberized ...

Notes

1. French Environment and Energy Management Agency (Ademe), (2016), 'Etude sur les Différentes Formes de Voitures de Transport avec Chauffeur'.
2. Hall, J. and Krueger, A. (2016), 'An analysis of the labor market for Uber's driver-partners in the United States', NBER Working Paper 22843.
3. Landier, A., Szomoru, D. and Thesmar, D. (2016), 'Travailler sur une plateforme Internet: une analyse des chauffeurs utilisant Uber en France', strategy report prepared for Uber.
4. Wallsten, S. (2015), 'The competitive effects of the sharing economy: how is Uber changing taxis?', Technology Policy Institute.
5. http://fivethirtyeight.com/features/uber-is-serving-new-yorks-outer-bor oughs-more-than-taxis-are/.
6. Ademe, 'Etude sur les Différentes Formes de Voitures de Transport avec Chauffeur', ibid.
7. www.businessinsider.com/uber-vs-taxi-pricing-by-city-2014–10?IR=T.
8. http://blog.eurecab.com/2015/04/taxis-g7-vs-uber-confrontation-de-deux-poids-lourds-du-taxi-et-du-vtc/.
9. www.nber.org/papers/w22627.
10. Chen, K. and Sheldon, M. (2015), 'Dynamic pricing in a labor market: surge pricing and flexible work on the Uber platform', UCLA Anderson working paper.

11. Brodeur, A. and Nield, K. (2016) 'Has Uber made it easier to get a ride in the rain?', Institute for the Study of Labour (IZA).
12. www.huffingtonpost.com/2014/12/15/uber-sydney-surge-pri cing_n_6325026.html.
13. http://bgr.com/2016/01/04/new-years-eve-uber-surge-pricing-reactions/.
14. www.leparisien.fr/espace-premium/paris-75/des-trajets-en-vtc-a-230-eur-la-nuit-du-reveillon-03-01-2015-4415551.php.
15. https://en.wikipedia.org/wiki/Ultimatum_game.
16. https://theconversation.com/uber-china-rachete-par-didi-chuxing-ou-le-qui-perd-gagne-de-la-plateforme-californienne-63917.
17. https://theconversation.com/uber-ou-comment-conquerir-une-position-dominante-mondiale-en-un-temps-record-48692.
18. 'Alphabet executive David Drummond leaves Uber board', *The Wall Street Journal*, 30 August 2016.
19. 'Uberworld: the race to reinvent transport', *The Economist*, 3 September 2016.

TWENTY FOUR

Intermezzo on the Redistributive Effects of Competition

Let's start this chapter with a slightly provocative question. Might competition actually have nothing to do with fairness? Indeed, from a theoretical standpoint there is nothing odd about such a question. Let's see why.

First of all, it is important to bear in mind that the key principle for economists, when appraising a situation, is to regard as optimal conditions under which no single individual can improve their welfare at the expense of another. If by my action I earn ten but you lose eleven then it should be stopped, for were it to continue, the wealth of society (reduced in the present case to just two individuals, you and me) would decrease. On the contrary, if through my action, you lose nine, I can make up for your loss, so my action deserves to be implemented.

Now economic theory demonstrates, on the basis of a set of assumptions that are of course restrictive, that trade under conditions of perfect competition always leads to this sort of optimal situation. Imagine for a moment a society consisting of individuals only concerned with their self-interest, immersed in an economy comprising competitive markets and endowed at the outset with a certain amount of wealth in the form of goods and money. As their needs and preferences differ, they exchange some of these goods on the basis of prices revealed by the markets; some of them will prosper, but none of them will be less well off. The overall wealth of society increases.

Note however that the situation, following competitive trade, may still be optimal, even if there is greater inequality. This would be the case, for instance, if it enabled those who are already richly endowed to improve their welfare, whereas the predicament of those who were least well off at the outset was no worse. Moreover, in the event of trade opening up several different ways of re-allocating wealth, the theory does not give preference to any particular outcome. It is neutral. Such indifference may bother you. However, the theory of competitive trade provides a good defence, demonstrating that any situation of distribution that is considered ideal may be achieved by markets in a state of perfect competition simply by playing on the initial endowment. If the situation after trade is unsatisfactory with regard to fairness, the solution is to redistribute the initial endowments before trade through pure transfers in such a way that subsequent trade produces the desired situation of fairness. Let's look at an example, in which we accept as a principle of fairness that no individual prefers what another receives to what they themselves have received. To arrive at a situation which fulfils this condition, all that is needed is to ensure that everyone initially has an equal share of the cake and then to allow trade to proceed. We assume of course that individuals have a heterogeneous appetite for the relevant cake. If they all attached the same value to the initial equal share of cake, there would be no trade. Trade only occurs because some individuals, the buyers, attach greater value to their share, and others, the sellers, attach less.

It is essential to be clear about what is meant by 'cake' here, given that the image crops up in all sorts of places. The rule governing how it is shared out is supposed to represent fairness – which is the concern of distributive justice. Its size, representing overall wealth, is the concern of competitive markets. Thanks to the defence mentioned above, the two can, in principle, be separated. A word of caution though: when we say that economics only concerns itself with the size of the cake and not the rules for its distribution, it would be a mistake to imagine that trade increases the physical size of the cake. If we gather up the various pieces of cake again, after they have been shared out, it will be the same size as it was at the outset! It is the value of the cake that varies, not its circumference or thickness. Supposing it was worth 100 before trade, when everyone held an equal share, it will be worth 120 afterwards, for the competitive market will have allocated a bigger share to those who like cake more than their fellows. In order to make the dimensions of the cake grow, within the framework of the simplified economy described above, we would have to add innovation or outside shocks. But that would further complicate matters.

I have just summarized a historical monument of economic thought, the General Equilibrium Theory and its theorems on Social Welfare. A Frenchman, Léon Walras, an American, Kenneth Arrow, and a Franco-American, Gérard Debreu, were the main architects of this edifice, which was completed in the 1960s. The admiration this monument inspires among economists explains the virtue they unquestioningly attribute to perfect competition. The inscription on the mausoleum asserts that it maximizes collective wealth by using and allocating resources in the best possible way, without anyone losing out (at least potentially, because their losses can always be compensated by transferring part of the winners' surplus).

But we may be dazzled or even blinded by such admiration. The virtue of perfect competition only expresses itself under certain conditions, particularly in the absence of negative externalities, such as pollution, or positive effects such as the use of networks and platforms. Another condition of perfect competition is the presence of diminishing returns. This deserves a closer look because it demolishes the theoretical defence for separating competition and fairness. (For readers wishing to enlarge their economic vocabulary, the official name of this defence is the second fundamental theorem of welfare economics.)

The diminishing-returns hypothesis means that the average unit cost will increase in line with the quantity produced. For example, it is necessary to dig increasingly deep to extract ore from a mine, so it costs more. Similarly, more marginal land must be used to produce more wheat, also increasing unit costs. However, in most industries, returns, at least initially, increase thanks to economies of scale, so the average unit cost will decrease as output rises. For instance, the more cars a company produces, the less they will cost. This holds true up to a certain point beyond which diseconomies of scale appear, for reasons of organization or disorganization such as congestion on car production lines. The competitive market is unable to cope with such diminishing returns, it no longer being possible to achieve a price, equilibrium or ideal re-allocation, even if the initial endowments are changed.

In more simple terms, the effectiveness of the defence can be questioned by arguing that the initial re-allocation required for the competitive market to attain an ideal situation with regard to fairness would be so radical, demanding such large transfers of resources in comparison with the original situation, as to be wholly impracticable legally and politically.[1]

Competition, even when it is perfect, cannot be considered to be neutral with regard to fairness.

Competition and Equality Between Consumers and Companies

Competition operates at three distinct levels: distributing the gains from trade between consumers and companies; sharing these gains between consumers themselves; and lastly, sharing profit between companies themselves. Let's look at the three effects, one after another.

Roughly speaking, a monopoly is fair to business, unfair to consumers. Put the opposite way, competition is unfair to business, fair to consumers. The reason is intuitive: in a monopoly situation, the company can set a higher price. Let us suppose that the decision for consumers hinges on purchasing a good, or not, rather than on how much of it they want. We can then focus on an initial situation of perfect competition. When the market becomes monopolistic, some consumers will stop buying the good because they can no longer afford it; the others will continue, but their gain, or surplus – equal to the difference between the price and the most they are willing to pay for the good – decreases. The loss incurred by the latter category ends up in the pockets of the monopoly in the form of profit. Generally speaking, when the monopoly, or 'market', power, of a company increases, a pure transfer effect operates between it and the consumers still buying its goods. Its gain is equal to their loss. On the other hand, it obviously does not gain what is lost by consumers no longer buying its goods. That is lost for everyone, which is precisely the drawback of a monopoly, setting aside issues of fairness, with no concern for the question of whether distribution of the surplus should primarily benefit shareholders or consumers.

However, the welfare loss, also known as deadweight loss, is only lost for everyone if the monopoly sets a single price. If, on the other hand, it were to set a price equal to each consumer's willingness to pay, it would sweep the board. Under these circumstances, none of the consumers would stop buying because the price quoted to them would be strictly equal to the upper limit of what they were ready to pay. In terms of distribution, a perfectly discriminating monopoly produces the exact opposite of perfect competition, maximizing profit for the company and leaving no gain whatsoever to consumers, instead of no profit at all and maximum gain. We should point out in passing that in this theoretical construct the difference between competition and monopoly relates exclusively to the share-out of the gain from trade between vendor and buyer, not to the amount of the gain from trade. In other words, the perfectly discriminating monopoly is just as effective as perfect competition when it comes to creating wealth. Above all, remember that perfect competition is synonymous with just one price for all buyers. Which brings us to equality between consumers.

That everyone should be charged the same price seems a very egalitarian situation. It involves no discrimination, be it social – relating to age, gender or place of birth, for instance – or economic – relating to income or property. Indeed it is often perceived as egalitarian, witness the public outbursts condemning discriminatory pricing systems in rail or air transport, or demands to maintain a single rate for gas or electricity set by central government. This stance is not without its contradictions, those who criticise different prices often being the first to criticise competition too. Perhaps it has not occurred to them that price discrimination is a way of getting closer to the utopian slogan: 'From each according to his ability . . .'

The levelling effect of competition may also be contrasted with the effect of co-operation in the case of rules for allocating a common cost, such as installing a lift in an old apartment block or building an airport runway. How should this cost be shared out fairly between the various users, in a way that covers the full cost and suits all parties? In formal terms, the answer to this question is unbelievably complex. It is based on sets of complicated, highly abstract axioms and on sophisticated games theory. I shall restrict myself to making three points. First, it is not always possible to fulfil all three conditions at the same time. One or another may have to be shelved. Second, egalitarian sharing stands little chance of being accepted by all parties, whether it concerns all the flat-owners in a block paying the same amount to fit a lift, regardless of which floor they live on, or airlines, some operating large planes that need long runways, others with small aircraft requiring much less space. In other words, the competitive market is unable to deliver stable allocation in such instances. Third, consensus building among users, not by setting a single price but through debate and firm commitments – in other words, co-operation – often yields more durable solutions. They are also more diverse, which is an advantage, for co-operation is better at adapting to suit the different social preferences of groups and communities.

Demands for uniformity often concern the quality of goods and services too. Some people assert that there should only be one level of quality. In keeping with this principle, everyone should, for instance, enjoy the same level of comfort in a train, the same after-sales guarantee for household goods, the same medical care in hospital. Diversity of supply may thus be perceived as a fault. It does not place consumers on an equal footing. In particular, high-earners would be able to buy goods beyond the reach of others. From this point of view, competition through monopoly or differentiation would be unfavourable, whereas perfect competition with wholly uniform products would be laudable. Here again it has to be said that those who condemn variety of supply are often fiercely critical of competition too. So it goes.

Competition and Inequality Between Companies

To conclude, let's look at the question of competition and equality between companies. The notion of equality between companies may come as a surprise, it being more commonly associated with people and citizens, than with profit-making organizations. However an entire legal framework also exists for business, its concerns ranging from freedom to trade to competition law. It governs the conditions of equality that prevail and must continue to prevail between them. But why is equality between companies important? Indeed, what does it mean and how does it relate to competition?

We may provide an initial answer to these three questions by looking at a very simple situation. Imagine a company in a monopoly position which prevents another company from entering its markets, for example, by threatening its management with retaliation or by wrecking its public image. In so doing, it is prohibiting another firm from sharing in its profits. (In passing, we should recall that it is not a straightforward two-way split, because the profit from a monopoly is greater than the sum of the profits for two firms in a duopoly.) By thwarting competition, over and above the prejudice to consumers due to higher prices, the monopolist deprives the other company of an opportunity.

So equality between companies above all means they should enjoy the same opportunities to develop. Freedom of enterprise and trade is essential here, enabling companies to enter any market they like. They can compete, striving to climb up the ranking just like Premier League football teams. Sticking with this sporting metaphor, we may add that the rules must be the same for everyone, not favouring one or another company but putting them all on an equal footing. In short, a level playing field. Changing ends at half-time, for instance, saves one team from playing the whole match on the bumpy part of the pitch or against a head wind.

The guarantee of equality between firms also means ensuring that those which prevail do so on their own merits, not by cheating. Similarly, those that fail do so because they perform less well, not because of the malpractice of their rivals. Cheating and malpractice may refer to actions, such as setting fire to a competitor's warehouse, that may be prosecuted under civil law, but also competition law. This specific legal framework is intended to maintain effective competition in the marketplace and ensure it is neither distorted nor impeded. There is no shortage of stock phrases for describing more or less the same thing that is the triptich: breaking up cartels, condemning abuse of a dominant position and forbidding mergers that impede competition.

Competition law is known to uphold consumer interests, prosecuting actions which lead to higher prices. But it also upholds the interests of companies, or at least a majority of them. This aspect is often disregarded or misunderstood. The root cause of such confusion is that firms frequently complain about competition. True enough it obliges them to make a constant effort to stay in the game – remember the Red Queen's race (see Chapter 18). For some of them, competition means suffering losses, laying off staff, closing factories, even bankruptcy and closure. Given that competition law exists to protect competition, it surely cannot be in the interests of business? QED.

This attitude overlooks the fact that competition also means that some companies succeed. Look, for example, at cartels. There is no doubt that firms signing a secret agreement to share a market would rather competition law was not enforced. Yet most cartels concern intermediate products such as cement. So cartel members sell their goods to other companies, which are penalized in the process. Furthermore, it may not be in the interests of more successful companies to join the cartel. But if they refuse they may be subjected to retaliation. The same is true of abuse of a dominant position. A company which ousts a competitor by temporarily cutting its prices to below its marginal cost is liable to prosecution under anti-trust law, leading to a heavy fine. Its competitors clearly benefit from the protection the law affords them against such practices. Companies whose projected merger is quashed by the European Commission or the United States Federal Trade Commission may complain bitterly, but in general their competitors are relieved. In short, prosecuting anti-competitive behaviour re-establishes a level playing field, giving companies the opportunity to succeed through their talents and merits.

All companies are obviously not equal with regard to skills and merits and the ones that do best open up a lead over less well endowed rivals. For example, when the market expands due to lower transaction or transport costs, the most successful companies will grow sales more than their competitors. They may contact and capture customers who were previously beyond their reach, due to the high cost of serving them. This will be detrimental to less efficient competitors, previously protected by distance and other obstacles to competition. Some will quite simply be knocked out of the market, whereas others will be doomed to stagnation. The effect of competition in this case is to increase concentration and inequality, in terms of size, between companies. Such disparity will often open up a gap in terms of productivity, investment, attractiveness and ultimately the profitability of rival companies.

The allusion to talent is by no means gratuitous. Economists, who have long taken an interest in superstars in the music industry, are now intrigued by how and why the phenomenon is spreading to industry as a whole.[2] The rise of superstar firms is a key topic in both academic journals and mainstream magazines.[3,4] The widening gap between such moguls and other companies is now well documented. Here are a few figures to illustrate this point: the top-100 US companies, ranked by sales, now account for half of the nation's gross domestic product, up from one-third in the 1994[5]; stock-exchange-listed companies in the USA reporting more than $1 billion in annual revenue currently account for 70% of overall profits, compared with 55% in 1993[6]; also in the USA, the profits of the top 0.1% of independent private companies have doubled since the 2000s, whereas performance at the bottom of the scale has not changed[7]; in France, the top-100 companies in terms of added value account for 22% of the total, a share which has risen since 1993[8]; lastly the productivity superstars – the fifty most efficient companies in each sector – in the twenty-three countries belonging to the Organization for Economic Cooperation and Development increased their lead by 30% in the 2000s.[9]

The growing inequality between companies deserves to be underlined because it causes other forms of inequality. The high profits of superstar firms benefit their shareholders, in other words wealthy households, for the latter often have substantial savings and financial assets, but penalize consumers, particularly low-income households which spend most of what they earn on consumer goods. Furthermore, the growing power of these giant firms contributes to wage inequality. It is a well established fact that the increasing disparity of wages observed since the 1980s has less to do with growing disparity between the employees of a specific company, between management and poorly qualified workers, and more to do with increasing wage disparity between companies, with high average pay in some cases, much lower in others.[10] Successful companies pay increasingly high wages, much as superstar football clubs such as Manchester United: the biggest gap is not between the best and least-well paid players of this Premier League club, or those of its rivals, rather between the average pay of first and second division players.

In this chapter, we have seen that competition goes hand-in-hand with various, powerful redistributive effects. On the whole they benefit consumers, but they may also reduce or increase inequality between them, to the advantage or disadvantage of the least well off. Furthermore, free, undistorted competition – to borrow a fine phrase from European Union competition law – penalizes some companies (which disregard anti-trust laws) and benefits others (which rely on their own merits). But if companies are free to capitalize on their talents, competition creates winners, such as the superstars that are currently flourishing, and losers, companies which for lack of investments, skills or quite simply good fortune, are losing ground.

The machinery of competition is blind, devoid of strategy or objective, with no guiding hand or signature, so its massive effects on inequality may give rise to anxiety and make the market seem a means of redress far inferior to public intervention. Providing of course one believes that the State only acts on redistribution for the benefit of those most in need.

Notes

1. Sen, A. (1993), 'Markets and freedoms: achievements and limitations of the market mechanism in promoting individual freedoms', *Oxford Economic Papers*, new series 45(4): 519–541.
2. Krueger, A. (2005), 'The economics of real superstars: the market for rock concerts in the material world,' *Journal of Labor Economics* 23(1): 1–30.

3. Autor, D., Dorn, D., Katz, L. F., Patterson C., and Van Reenen, J. (2017), 'The fall of the labor share and the rise of superstar firms', London School of Economics Centre for Economic Performance discussion paper 1482.
4. 'The rise of the superstars', *The Economist*, 17 September 2016.
5. Flowers, A. 'Big business is getting bigger', *FiveThirtyEight*, 18 May 2015.
6. www.mckinsey.com/mgi/overview/in-the-news/playing-to-win-the-new-global-competition-for-corporate-profits.
7. Smith, M., Yagan, D., Zidar, O. and Zwick, E. (2017), 'Capitalists in the twenty-first century', University of California at Berkeley and University of Chicago working paper.
8. Giovanni, J. Di, Levchenko, A. and Mejean, I. (2017), 'Large firms and international business cycle comovement', *American Economic Review* 107(5): 598–602.
9. Andrews, D., Criscuolo, C. and Gal, P. N. (2015), 'Frontier firms, technology diffusion and public policy: micro-evidence from OECD countries', OECD Main Background Papers.
10. Bloom, N., Guvenen, F., Price, D. J., Song, J. and Von Wachter, T. (2015), 'Firming up inequality', National Bureau of Economic Research working paper 21199.

CONCLUSION

The Changing Face of Competition Today

At the beginning of this book, we asked whether competition now differs from the past, say before 1980. The subsequent chapters have highlighted many changes: the growing speed with which firms achieve global dominance; the fact that such global dominance, once restricted to mineral and agricultural raw materials, now reaches into many other sectors; the boom in mega-firms marketing a huge range of products, variants and brands; the multiplication and importance of business ecosystems and other types of alliance between firms; the creation of new markets by business – from auctions to trading platforms; the swift demise of whole swathes of industry and the sudden obsolescence of products. But is this new apparel sufficient for us to conclude that competition is not what it used to be, that it is all new, from head to toe?

The Same Factors Still at Work but More Forcibly

The same key factors – market extension and innovation, particularly in technology – are still driving and consolidating changes in competition. Bigger markets mean more companies are competing, making similar products for the same customer base. Meanwhile, new technology is disturbing incumbents by offering new goods and services. These trends have gathered momentum since the 1980s.

Increasingly rapid spread of markets

The increasingly rapid spread of markets is due to the reduction in transport costs and transaction costs, such as obtaining information and contracting expenses. But it is also the result of political decisions, such as market deregulation and lower customs duty. Since the end of the 1970s, these key factors have contributed to extending markets.

Transport costs have fallen rapidly, helped by lower oil prices. At the same time, transaction costs have substantially dropped thanks to the development of information and communications technology.

We should also bear in mind that the late 1970s saw the start of a new phase of globalization. The four Asian Tigers – Hong Kong, Singapore, South Korea and Taiwan – started catching up with the industrialized countries. When Deng Xiaoping returned to power and the first special economic zones were established, China began to prepare for a new role in world trade. Government policies designed to deregulate the economy and break up cartels also contributed to a larger trend. In 1984, the American telecommunications mogul AT&T was split up, after lengthy anti-trust proceedings. Margaret Thatcher and Ronald Reagan, elected in 1979 and 1980 respectively, advocated liberalization of network industries. Similar moves followed, and the operation of electricity and gas networks, railway systems and aviation was in due course opened up to competition in many parts of the world. At about the same time, efforts to combat cartels – monopolies comprising several players – were stepped up. In 1978, in a drive to uncover secret agreements between competitors, the US authorities introduced leniency programmes to encourage companies to report their own malpractice and provide information on other members of the cartel in which they were involved. Other countries then followed suit and the financial sanctions imposed on cartels increased.

Accelerating innovation

Three general-purpose technologies have appeared, one after another, since the late 1970s: personal computing, the Internet and smartphones. The power of the oldest technology has been compared to that of electricity. The second one enabled the development of online trading and publicity, giving rise to giants such as Amazon, Facebook and Google. The third, most recent arrival still holds considerable potential for further innovation.

With competition between Apple's iOS and Google's Android we have seen that general-purpose technology is a form of innovation, that irrigates and transforms the entire economy, much as the steam engine. Primarily, such technology gives rise to applications in most industrial and service sectors, steadily improving over time and facilitating the emergence of a large number of disruptive innovations, which augment its overall effect. These characteristics are part of a virtuous circle. The development of applications is an incentive for continuous improvement of the core technology; such improvements reduce the cost of applications for end-users and lead to additional innovations, broadening the outlets for the technology in other fields and speeding up the pace of innovation. Personal computing is a good example of this dynamic. The PC became affordable in the 1980s and was massively adopted in business and homes, lending itself to a wide range of uses, from games to spreadsheets, through word processing and email. Over the past thirty years, its performance has improved beyond recognition, its price has dropped substantially and its software has made dozens of products obsolete, witness the word processor which put an end to typewriters.

More or Less Intense Competition?

So, by taking 1980 as our baseline, the forces acting on competition appear more powerful than before. But does this mean that the nature of competition itself has changed, gaining in intensity.

Its nature has not changed, in the sense that competition still takes the same forms. Its new apparel fits the same figure. Competition through innovation does not date from the past few decades. Even the forms only recently conceptualized by economic theory have existed for a long time: two-sided markets did not appear with electronic platforms such as Airbnb; newspapers have been competing for years to attract readers and advertisers, the two sides of their publicity market; nor is there anything new in the notion of an exchange. On the other hand, two forms of competition have undoubtedly become predominant, powered by disruptive innovation and hyper-differentiation.

Has the intensity of competition changed? Is it greater or lesser than in the past? It appears to be more powerful, with the dizzy turmoil of its constantly changing disguise, like some magician who in a flash can change costume onstage. But if we look more closely it is extremely difficult to provide an answer. Let's step back and think about what we've learnt in this book.

Signs of diminishing competition

We have seen that competition operates over a specific territory and for a given good or service. It depends on many parameters such as economies of scale, technological or regulatory barriers to entry, the diversity of consumer preferences, or the cost of transport in relation to the value of the good. However, variations in these parameters can only be gauged within the bounds of clearly delimited markets. We have identified and described them in a number of cases, ranging from twenty-foot containers to smartphone operating systems through gyms. This sample is of course remarkably small, there being innumerable markets the world over. We cannot generalize on the basis of just a few cases, however emblematic they may be. To quote the title of a recent book, let's just say that it is 'probably approximately correct' to assert, on the basis of the very small number of cases examined in this book, that competition is running out of steam.[1]

We would reach the same conclusion if we restricted ourselves to the United States. So let's take a closer look at that particular territory. Three key indirect indicators confirm the view that competition is being eroded there: corporate profits, the number of new entrants and concentration.[2]

The liquid assets of US firms as a percentage of gross domestic product has risen from under 1% in 1980 to over 5% in 2014. Over the same period, the return on invested capital increased from 8% to 16%. Recent econometric research also shows that markups (the price divided by the cost) have substantially increased since the early 1980s.[3] These profit indicators suggest that the situation has never been as favourable for US firms and their shareholders, prompting some commentators to speak of an age of hyper-profits.[4]

Turning to industrial demographics, the number of new companies entering the market every year has been dropping since 1980. Moreover, every year since 2008, the number of existing businesses that have stopped trading has exceeded the number of new enterprises. The decline in entrepreneurship affects all sectors. Surprisingly, IT startups are no exception to this rule.[5] The trend is not restricted to just 'mom and pop' neighbourhood shops or services (often launched by people trying to escape unemployment or improve their lot). Everyone is struggling to find a place in the sun, out of the giant shadow cast by such as Walmart or Amazon.

Sectoral studies have provided most of the data showing that concentration is growing too. It is a well-established fact in financial services, food and hospitals, for example. But a few indicators suggest that it is a more widespread trend. According to the US Census Bureau, the nation's top-50 firms increased their share of overall sales in seven out of ten macro-sectors. Drawing on more detailed data from this agency, *The Economist* reported that in two-thirds of industrial sectors, the four leading corporations increased their relative market share in 1997–2012. On average by 15%.[6]

Taken as a whole, these data suggest that the monopoly power of US companies has increased in the past few decades, a trend that worries some observers, including free-market advocates. Witness the titles of recent publications condemning what is increasingly seen as excessive market power: The oligopoly problem[7]; Monopoly's new era[8]; The rise of market power[9]; America needs a giant dose of competition.[10]

Ambiguous effects

In the absence of any definite proof, backed by observation, that competition is weakening, we may be able to derive some insights from its causes and effects.

Let's start with the extension of markets. At first sight, this trend leads to more intense competition, prompting the entry of new players previously too remote to intervene. Moreover, if we extrapolate to the markets in general what we know specifically about international trade, the new players are mainly manufacturers of substitutes. Competition here is head-on, between local and distant production capacity. International trade over the past thirty years has mainly been driven by existing products. Washing machines, anthracite, ethylene glycol and even umbrella ribs are among the goods for which trade has increased spectacularly between 1992 and 2007.[11] Over the same period, new products, such as laptop computers, airbags for cars or cellphones, only accounted for about a quarter of the growth in world trade. So apparently, far from slackening, competition has stiffened.

However, such categorical certainties crumble if we bear in mind that market extension is not only a matter of supply. Demand has substantially increased too. Between 1990 and 2010, the planet gained 1.2 billion new consumers and those who were already consuming in the 1980s enjoyed greater purchasing power. So, although there are more companies competing in the enlarged markets, there are also more consumers to serve. The two trends have potentially contrary effects on the intensity of competition. Moreover greater demand justifies the construction of bigger production units to capitalize on economies of scale. Companies which, for one reason or another, have failed to grow are sidelined or eliminated, leading in turn to more concentrated production, an additional factor that potentially saps competition. Lastly, as we well know, individual preferences differ so a large consumer base enables firms to differentiate their products even more. The massive differentiation we are currently seeing in final consumer goods is in itself a force dulling competition.

The effects of innovation, making competition more or less intense, are just as ambiguous. On the one hand, it has undoubtedly boosted competition. New technology has given countless entrepreneurs an opportunity to enter markets previously closed to them. In response, many incumbents have also entered the race to improve their competitive edge through innovation. But on the other hand, shifts in technology have given rise to a larger number of markets shielded by intellectual property rights, network effects or barriers to entry linked to research and development. Does headlong innovation cause profits to diverge, with a substantial increase in the gains of efficient firms, enabling them in turn to defend their position against competitors, doomed to stagnation?

What is more, market extension and accelerating innovation have both contributed to the growth of superstar corporations. These firms have increased their lead over other companies and now occupy well established dominant positions, so impregnable that we may wonder if they will one day be challenged by new-comers. Who, in the last analysis, will be proved right? The Austrian economist Joseph Schumpeter, who foresaw a succession of temporary monopolies, or the French political thinker Pierre-Joseph Proudhon, who asserted that 'competition kills competition'?[12]

Concluding this review of the current state of affairs, we are not in a position to come down firmly on one or other side regarding an average or general trend, based on either inductive or deductive reasoning. My own impression is that competition is definitely losing momentum, but the reader may well reach another conclusion. We are all affected differently by changes in competition, depending on whether our perception is that of a consumer, an employee in an endangered company, an executive in a robust firm or indeed a budding entrepreneur. Such effects, experienced at first hand, necessarily leave different impressions. Regardless of where you stand, what matters is that this book should have opened your eyes to the diversity of contemporary competition and the subtleties of how it works. I hope too that it has broadened your outlook, reaching beyond an all-too-frequent moral stance on this topic, and that it has given you a grasp of why real-life competition is very different from the theoretical model of its 'perfect' counterpart. A difference that is actually of very little concern, for, much as Andersen's tale of The Emperor's New Clothes, perfect competition is only a fable.

Notes

1. Valiant, L. (2013), *Probably Approximately Correct: Nature's Algorithms for Learning and Prospering in a Complex World*, New York City, NY: Basic Books.
2. Competition Issue Brief, White House Council of Economic Advisers, Washington DC, 14 April 2016.
3. Barkai, S. (2017), 'Declining labor and capital shares', London Business School; Eeckhout, J. and De Loecker, J. (2017), 'The rise of market power and the macroeconomic implications', NBER working paper 23687.

4. 'The problem with profits. Big firms in the United States have never had it so good. Time for more competition', *The Economist*, 26 March 2016.
5. Decker, R. et al. (2014), 'The secular decline in business dynamism in the US', University of Maryland Department of Economics working paper.
6. 'The problem with profits', *The Economist*.
7. Wu, T. 'The oligopoly problem', *The New Yorker*, 15 April 2013.
8. Stiglitz, J. E. (2016), 'Monopoly's new era', *Project Syndicate*.
9. Eeckhout, and De Loecker. 'The rise of market power and the macroeconomic implications', ibid.
10. 'Too much of a good thing, profits are too high. America needs a giant dose of competition', *The Economist*, 26 March 2016.
11. World Trade Report 2013: Factors shaping the future of world trade, World Trade Organization.
12. Proudhon, P-J. (1846), *Systèmes des Contradictions Economiques ou Philosophie de la Misère*, Paris: Guillaumin et Compagnie.

Index